The
Mumps
Programming
Language

by

Kevin C. Ó Kane, Ph.D.
Professor Emeritus
Department of Computer Science
The University of Northern Iowa
Cedar Falls, Iowa 50614-0507

kc.okane@gmail.com
http://www.cs.uni.edu/~okane/
http://threadsafebooks.com/

For other works by this author on Amazon:
Omaha
IBM Mainframe Assembly Language
The Constitutional Convention of 2022

Threadsafe Publishing & Railway Maintenance Co.
Hyannis, Nebraska

Cover: *Section of the MeSH Hierarchy*
Some artwork within is based on the National Library of
Medicine Medical Subject Headings (MeSH):
http://www.nlm.nih.gov/mesh/

Revised: May 10, 2016

Contents

1 The Mumps Language..**9**

1.1 History and Background......................................9
1.2 Current Implementations.................................14
   1.2.1 Fidelity Information Services' GT.M.................14
   1.2.2 InterSystems Caché..............................15
   1.2.3 An Open Source Implementation by Ray Newman.........15
   1.2.4 GPL Mumps.....................................16

2 Data Types..**17**

2.1 Variables..18
2.2 Arrays...19
2.3 Local Arrays...20
2.4 Global Arrays..20
   2.4.1 Naked Global References.........................26
2.5 Environments...26
2.6 Collating Sequences....................................26

3 The Basics..**29**

3.1 Mumps Expression Precedence............................30
3.2 Mumps Commands..31
3.3 Creating and Assigning Values to Variables.............32
3.4 Scope of Variables.....................................33

4 Overview of Commands and Concepts.......................**35**

4.1 The Set Command..35
   4.1.1 Operators......................................35
4.2 Input/Output...36
   4.2.1 I/O Format Control Codes........................36
   4.2.2 The Read Command...............................36
   4.2.3 The Write Command..............................37
4.3 The If Command...37
   4.3.1 Logical Operators..............................39
   4.3.2 Relational Operators...........................39
4.4 Blocks...40
4.5 The For Command..42
4.6 Input/Output Units.....................................45
4.7 Post-Conditionals......................................47
4.8 Navigating Arrays.....................................49
4.9 Command line parameters................................51
4.10 Indirection...51
4.11 Subroutines and Parameter Passing.....................53
   4.11.1 Subroutines Invoked by Do or Goto.............53
   4.11.2 Extrinsic Functions and Extrinsic Variables......56

5 Mumps Operators...**59**

5.1 Assignment operator (=)...............................59
5.2 Arithmetic unary operators: (+, -)....................59
5.3 Arithmetic binary operators: (+, -, *, /, \, #, **)....59

5.4 Arithmetic relational operators: (>, <, '>, '<)....................60
5.5 String binary operator: (_)..60
5.6 String relational operators: = [ ] ? '? '= '[']]] ']].................60
5.7 Pattern match operator...61
5.8 Logical operators: &, ! '...62
5.9 The indirection operator: @..62

6 Commands...65

6.1 break (abbreviation: b)...65
6.2 close (abbreviation: c)..67
6.3 do (abbreviation: d)...67
   6.3.1 Do without Arguments (abbreviation: d)..............................67
   6.3.2 do with arguments..69
      6.3.2.1 do with a Label Argument..69
      6.3.2.2 do with Label and Parameters...................................71
6.4 else (abbreviation: e)...72
6.5 for (abbreviation: f)...72
6.6 goto (abbreviation: g)..74
6.7 halt (abbreviation: h)..74
6.8 hang (abbreviation: h)...74
6.9 if (abbreviation: i)..75
6.10 job (abbreviation: j)..76
6.11 kill (abbreviation: k)...77
6.12 lock (abbreviation: l)...77
6.13 merge (abbreviation: m)..78
6.14 new (abbreviation: n)..78
6.15 open (abbreviation: o)...80
6.16 quit (abbreviation: q)..81
6.17 read (abbreviation: r)..83
6.18 set (abbreviation: s)..85
6.19 tcommit (abbreviation: tc)..85
6.20 trestart (abbreviation: tre).......................................86
6.21 trollback (abbreviation: tro).....................................86
6.22 tstart (abbreviation: ts)...86
6.23 use (abbreviation: u)...86
6.24 view (abbreviation: v)...86
6.25 write (abbreviation: w)..87
6.26 xecute (abbreviation: x)...87

7 Builtin/Intrinsic Variables.................................89

7.1 $device (abbreviation: $d)...89
7.2 $ecode (abbreviation: $ec)..89
7.3 $estack (abbreviation: $es).......................................89
7.4 $etrap (abbreviation: $et)...89
7.5 $horolog (abbreviation: $h).......................................89
7.6 $io (abbreviation: $i)..89
7.7 $job (abbreviation: $j)..89
7.8 $key (abbreviation: $k)..90
7.9 $principal (abbreviation: $p)......................................90
7.10 $quit (abbreviation: $q)...90

7.11 $stack (abbreviation: $st)..90
7.12 $storage (abbreviation: $s)..90
7.13 $system (abbreviation: $sy)..90
7.14 $test (abbreviation: $t)...90
7.15 $tlevel (abbreviation: $tl)...90
7.16 $trestart (abbreviation: $tr)...90
7.17 $x...90
7.18 $y...91
7.19 $z...91

8 Structured System Variables..93

8.1 ^$character (abbreviation: ^$c)..93
8.2 ^$device (abbreviation: ^$d)..93
8.3 ^$global (abbreviation: ^$g)...93
8.4 ^$job (abbreviation: ^$j)..93
8.5 ^$lock (abbreviation: ^$l)..93
8.6 ^$routine (abbreviation: ^$r)...93
8.7 ^$system (abbreviation: ^$s)...93
8.8 ^$z[...]..93

9 Builtin Functions...95

9.1 $ascii(e1) or $ascii(e1,i2)...95
9.2 $char(i1) or $char(i1,i2) or $char(i1,i2,...)......................95
9.3 $data(vn)...95
9.4 $extract(e1,i2) or $extract(e1,i2,i3)................................95
9.5 $find(e1,e2) or $find(e1,e2,i3)...96
9.6 $fnumber(numexp,code[,int])..96
9.7 $get(i1) or $get(i1,i2)...97
9.8 $justify(e1,i2) or $justify(e1,i2,i3)..................................97
9.9 $len(e1) or $len(e1,e2)..97
9.10 $name(vn[,count])...97
9.11 $next(vn) (deprecated)..98
9.12 $order(vn[,d])..98
9.13 $piece(e1,e2,i3) or $piece(e1,e2,i3,i4)...........................99
9.14 $qlength(e1)..100
9.15 $qsubscript(e1,e2)..100
9.16 $query(e1)..100
9.17 $random(i1)..102
9.18 $reverse(i1)..102
9.19 $select(t1:e1,t2:e2,...tn:en)...102
9.20 $translate(S1,S2) or $translate(S1,S2,S3).....................102

10 Programming Examples..105

10.1 The Medical Subject Headings (MeSH) Example............105
10.2 Building a MeSH Structured Global Array.....................106
10.3 Displaying the MeSH Global Array Part I.......................109
10.4 Printing the MeSH Global Array Part II...........................111
10.5 Displaying Global Arrays in Key Order...........................111
10.6 KWIC Index..113
10.7 Document-Term Matrix..117

11 Error Handling and Messages..................................**123**

Illustration Index

Figure 1 Early Mumps Systems Memory Layout..11
Figure 2 Example Strings..17
Figure 3 String Arithmetic..18
Figure 4 Truth Values of Strings...18
Figure 5 Local Arrays..20
Figure 6 Global Array Tree...21
Figure 7 Global Arrays...21
Figure 8 Global Array with Null Data..22
Figure 9 Global Data Only at Leaf Nodes...23
Figure 10 MeSH Tree as a Global Array...23
Figure 11 C Matrix...23
Figure 12 Global Data at Several Levels...24
Figure 13 Sparse Global Array...24
Figure 14 Global Array Indices..24
Figure 15 Global Array Examples...25
Figure 16 Table of Mumps Commands...32
Figure 17 Expressions..33
Figure 18 Read/Write Format Codes...36
Figure 19 Write Examples...37
Figure 20 If Without Arguments..39
Figure 21 $Test With Argumentless If..39
Figure 22 Relational Operators..40
Figure 23 Using Relational Operators..40
Figure 24 Blocks...41
Figure 25 Blocks with If and Else...41
Figure 26 Multi-level Blocks..41
Figure 27 $Test with Blocks...42
Figure 28 $Test without Blocks..42
Figure 29 For Command Examples..43
Figure 30 Nested For Loops..43
Figure 31 Quit with Block Example...44
Figure 32 Quit in an Iterative Block..44
Figure 33 Quit in a Nested Block..45
Figure 34 Open and Close Commands...46
Figure 35 Open Command...46
Figure 36 Post-conditionals...48
Figure 37 Using If/Else in Loops..49
Figure 38 Navigating Global Arrays..50
Figure 39 Command Line Parameters...51
Figure 40 Operator Indirection..52
Figure 41 Command Indirection...52
Figure 42 Do Command Examples...55
Figure 43 Extrinsics...56
Figure 44 Example Unary Operators...59
Figure 45 Binary Arithmetic Operators...60
Figure 46 Relational Operators..60
Figure 47 Negated Relationals...60
Figure 48 String Binary Operator..60
Figure 49 Equality Relational Operators...60
Figure 50 Contains Operator...61
Figure 51 Follows Operator..61
Figure 52 Pattern Match Codes...61
Figure 53 Example Pattern Matching..62
Figure 54 Logical Operators...62
Figure 55 Negated Operators...62
Figure 56 Indirection Example...63
Figure 57 Indirection with $Order()...63
Figure 58 GPL Mumps Break Examples..66
Figure 59 GPL Mumps Break Examples..66
Figure 60 GPL Mumps Break Examples..66
Figure 61 Close Examples...67
Figure 62 Do with No Arguments..68
Figure 63 Do with Multiple Blocks...68
Figure 64 Do With If...68
Figure 65 Do With Else...69
Figure 66 Do Effect on $Test..69
Figure 67 Do with Label Argument..70

Figure 68 Do with a File..70
Figure 69 Do with Indirection..70
Figure 70 Do with Parameters...71
Figure 71 For Examples..73
Figure 72 Goto Arguments..74
Figure 73 If Examples..76
Figure 74 if With $test...76
Figure 75 If With Else..76
Figure 76 Merge Examples..79
Figure 77 New Examples..80
Figure 78 Open Examples...81
Figure 79 Quit Examples..81
Figure 80 More Quit Examples...82
Figure 81 Quit in a Do Block...82
Figure 82 Iterative Do Block..82
Figure 83 Quit with Remote Block..82
Figure 84 Iterative Remote Block...83
Figure 85 Use Examples...86
Figure 86 Write Examples...87
Figure 87 Xecute Example..87
Figure 88 $Ascii() Examples...95
Figure 89 $Char() Examples...95
Figure 90 $Data() Examples...95
Figure 91 $Extract() Examples..96
Figure 92 $Find() Examples..96
Figure 93 $Fnumber() Format Codes..97
Figure 94 $Justify() Examples...97
Figure 95 $Len() Examples...97
Figure 96 $Name() Examples..98
Figure 97 $Order() Examples..99
Figure 98 $Piece() Examples...100
Figure 99 $Qlength() Examples..100
Figure 100 $Qsubscript() Examples..100
Figure 101 $Query() Examples...101
Figure 102 $Reverse() Examples..102
Figure 103 $Select() Example..102
Figure 104 $Translate() Examples..103
Figure 105 Sample MeSH Hierarchy..105
Figure 106 Global Array Commands..106
Figure 107 MeSH Global Array...107
Figure 108 Creating the Mesh tree..108
Figure 109 Print the MeSH tree..109
Figure 110 Printed Mesh tree...111
Figure 111 Alternate MeSH Tree Print..111
Figure 112 Alternative MeSH Print..112
Figure 113 MeSH Global Array Codes..113
Figure 114 Print MeSH Global..113
Figure 115 MeSH Global Printed...114
Figure 116 KWIC Example...117
Figure 117 Doc-Term Matrix (Image)...117
Figure 118 Document Indexing...122
Figure 119 Mumps Standard Error Codes...124
Figure 120 GPL Error Codes..124

1 The Mumps Language

1.1 History and Background

Mumps (**M**assachusetts General Hospital **U**tility **M**ulti-programming **S**ystem) is a general purpose programming language environment that provides ACID (Atomic, Consistent, Isolated, and Durable) database access by means of program level subscripted arrays and variables. The Mumps database allows schema-less, key-value access to disk resident data organized as trees that may also be viewed as sparse multi-dimensional arrays

Beginning in 1966, Mumps (also referred to as *M*), was developed by Neil Pappalardo and others in Octo Barnett's lab at the Massachusetts General Hospital (MGH) on a PDP-7, the same architecture on which Unix was being implemented at approximately the same time.

Initial experience with Mumps was very positive and it soon was ported to a number of other architectures including the PDP-11, the VAX, Data General, Prime, and, eventually, Intel x86 based systems, among others. It quickly became the basis for many early applications of computers to the health sciences.

When Mumps was originally designed, there were very few general database systems in existence. The origin of the term 'database' itself dates from this period. Such systems as existed, were mainly *ad hoc* application specific implementations that were neither portable nor extensible. The notion of a general purpose database design was just developing.

One of the first attempts to implement of a general purpose database system was GE/Honeywell's initial IDS - Integrated Data Store - which was developed in the mid-60s. Experience with this system lead to the subsequent organization and creation of the CODASYL DBTG (Committee on Data Systems Languages - DataBase Task Group) whose Network Model database was proposed (1969).

The Network Model was very complex and was implemented, in varying degrees, by only a few vendors. All of these were mainframe based. Most notable of these were GE/Honeywell's IDS/2, Cullinet's Integrated Database Management System (IDMS), Univac's DMS-1100, and Digital Equipment Corporation's DEC-10 based DBMS32.

At about the same time, IBM's IMS (Information Management System), was being developed in connection with the NASA Apollo program. It was first placed into service in 1968 running on IBM 360 mainframes. IMS, which is still in use today, is, like Mumps, hierarchical in structure.

The table based relational database model was initially proposed by E. F. Codd in 1970 but it wasn't until 1974 that IBM began to develop System R, the first system to utilize the model, as a research project. The first commercially available relational database system was released by Oracle in 1979.

In late 1960s mini-computers, although expensive, were becoming more widely available but they were still mainly confined to dedicated, mostly laboratory, applications. The operating systems available on these systems were primitive and, for the most part, single user. On many, the user was the operating system, flipping switches to manually install boot code, and loading compilers, linkers and programs from paper or magnetic tape.

DEC's RSX-11, the first commercial multi-user system on the PDP-11, was introduced in 1972. RSTS/E, a time sharing system mainly used for time-shared BASIC language programming, was implemented in 1970. Language support was likewise limited to a small set of languages such as FORTRAN, BASIC and Assembly Language. Although Unix existed at this time, it was not available outside AT&T until 1984.

Thus, in 1966 when the PDP-7 arrived at MGH, it had very little in the way of software, operating system or database support. So, as there were few options available, they started from scratch and designed Mumps to be not only a multi-user operating system, but also a language, and a database all in one.

For their database design, they developed a hierarchical model as this closely matched the tree structured nature of the medical record. To represent database trees in the language, they decided to use array references where each successive array index was part of a path description from the root of the array to intermediate and terminal nodes. They called these disk resident structures *global arrays*.

While in those days, Mumps, out of necessity, was its own standalone operating system, this is not the case today where Mumps programs run in Unix, Linux, OS/X, and Windows based environments.

The early Mumps operating system divided the very limited memory available on early mini-computers into small partitions, each assigned to a separate user. The system allocated and managed the memory partitions and granted time-slices to each user partition in a round-robin protocol. The Mumps operating system itself provided the Mumps language interpreter (Mumps was not compiled), centralized I/O, and managed access to the hierarchical database through a centralized Global Array File Manager, as outlined in Figure 1.

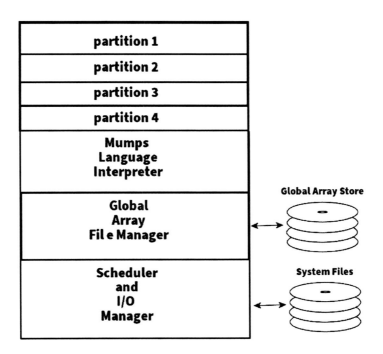

Figure 1 Early Mumps Systems Memory Layout

Memory partitions on these early machines were small, sometimes only a few thousand characters. Mumps programs were loaded into these as source code rather than as compiled binary. This was done because it was determined that compiled Mumps programs would be far larger than the corresponding source code versions, especially if the source code employed size reducing abbreviations for commands and functions. The increased overhead due to program interpretation was more than offset by the savings in overhead and improvement in response that a larger number of resident source code partitions would realize versus a smaller number of faster but frequently paged binary partitions.

Another reason for using source code was due to the fact that Mumps applications were (and are) large libraries of small, disk resident functional modules. Thus, since it took less time to load a small routine from disk than a larger binary module, performance and response time was improved. As an added benefit, small source code modules used less disk space which, at the time, was very expensive.

Finally, as Mumps programs, because they are database applications, were (and are) I/O intensive. Since all database I/O was centralized in the global array file manager, most Mumps programs, most of the time, whether compiled or interpreted, were (are) in a global file manager I/O wait state where there is, obviously, no penalty for interpretation.

The legacy of small memory machines can still be seen to this day, as Mumps programmers tend to abbreviate their code, sometimes excessively, although the original reason for doing this is long past.

Because of its simplicity, low cost and ease of use, Mumps quickly became popular and was used in many medical applications. COSTAR (COmputer-STored Ambulatory Record), for example, was a medical record, fiscal management and reporting system, developed in the mid-1970s for use in ambulatory care settings and it was widely used worldwide.

Today, Mumps programs are employed extensively in financial and clinical applications. If you've been to a doctor, been seen at a hospital, or used an ATM machine, your data has probably been processed by a Mumps program.

Mumps programs are the basis of the U.S. Veterans Administration's computerized medical record system VistA (*Veterans Health Information Systems and Technology Architecture*), the largest of its kind in the world. VistA is a collection of 80 different software subsystems that support the largest medical records system in the United States. It supports the medical records of over 8 million veterans, is used by 180,000 medical staff at 163 hospitals, more than 800 clinics, and 135 nursing homes.

Mumps is used by many health care organizations including Allscripts, Epic, Coventry Healthcare, EMIS, Partners HealthCare (including Massachusetts General Hospital), MEDITECH, GE Healthcare (formerly IDX Systems and Centricity), Sunquest Information Systems, DASA, Quest Diagnostics, and Dynacare, among others.

Some of the largest and most well known hospitals use Mumps based electronic health records systems. These include Kaiser Permanente, Cleveland Clinic, Johns Hopkins Medicine Hospitals, UCLA Health, Texas Health Resources, Massachusetts General Hospital, Mount Sinai Health System in New York City and the Duke University Health System.

Among financial, institutions it is used by Ameritrade, the Bank of England and Barclays Bank, as well as others.

What, after so many years, makes Mumps still popular in such demanding application areas? Mumps has remained viable by providing:

- In addition to sequential and direct file access, Mumps also implements, as an integral part of the language, a hierarchical and multi-dimensional database paradigm. When viewed as trees, data nodes can addressed as path descriptions in a manner which is easy for a novice programmer to master in a relatively short time. Alternatively, the trees can be viewed as sparse n-dimensional matrices of effectively unlimited size.

- Mumps supports built-in string manipulation operators and functions that provide programmers with access to efficient methods to accomplish complex string manipulation and pattern matching operations.

- Mumps runs on inexpensive, commodity servers and is easily scaled as demand grows.

- Mumps can handle Big Data quantities of information that are beyond the capabilities of many RDBMS systems with very high levels of performance and throughput.

- Mumps is very easily managed without the need for database administrators.

- Mumps databases are ACID (Atomicity, Consistency, Isolation, Durability) Compliant.

Syntactically, Mumps is based on an earlier language named JOSS and has an appearance similar to early versions of BASIC which is also said to be have been influenced by JOSS.

A feature of Mumps, noted above, which distinguished it from other language environments at the time was its ability to run multiple applications and serve multiple users concurrently on very primitive computers not mainframes.

Over the years, a number of implementations were developed. Many of these are now extinct or have evolved considerably from their original base. As the early implementations began to differ linguistically from on another, an effort to standardize Mumps began. This culminated in the 1977 ANSI standard for Mumps (X11.1-1977).

The standards effort continued until 1995 when the last standard was published (see: *American National Standard for Information Systems - Programming Languages - M ANSI/MDC X11.1-1995*). Since then, the standards writing Mumps Development Committee has disbanded and there have been no new standards developed. At present, the 1995 standard has lapsed in the United States but remains in effect at ISO (ISO/IEC 11756:1999). Also, as of 1995, there were related and proposed standards either published or in development for Mumps system interconnections (X11.2), a graphical kernel definition (X11.3), X-window binding (X11.4), TCP-IP binding (X11.5) and a windowing API (X11.6). These have also lapsed in the United Sates but some are still in effect at ISO. Some of the recommendations in these have been incorporated in some implementations. Also, Mumps transaction processing commands and functions were new in 1995 and not well defined. Since then, most vendors have implemented their own transaction processing procedures and commands and these will vary from one to another. You should consult your vendor's manual for details.

1.2 Current Implementations

Mumps (also referred to as **M**) is a simple, easily learned, powerful database scripting and string manipulation language which is ideal for both desktop and server applications. In the words of the 1995 Standard M Pocket Guide, Mumps is "... *an imperative (command oriented), dynamic, late-binding language oriented toward manipulation of strings and sparse arrays with string subscripts.*"

Each implementation of Mumps has added a number of additional commands and functions not found in the original standard. While many of these are similar across most implementations, their specific names and parameters differ. You should consult your implementation's user manual for details.

At one time, there were many implementations of Mumps available but, at present, this has consolidated to just a few and include the following:

1.2.1 Fidelity Information Services' GT.M

From the FIS web site:

> *GT.M™ Database Engine with Extreme Scalability and Robustness*
>
> *GT.M is a database engine with scalability proven in the largest real-time core processing systems in production at financial institutions worldwide, as well as in large, well known healthcare institutions, but with a small footprint that scales down to use in small clinics, virtual machines and software appliances.*
>
> *The GT.M data model is a hierarchical associative memory (i.e., multi-dimensional array) that imposes no restrictions on the data types of the indexes and the content - the application logic can impose any schema, dictionary or data organization suited to its problem domain.* GT.M's compiler for the standard M (also known as MUMPS) scripting language implements full support for ACID (Atomic, Consistent, Isolated, Durable) transactions, using optimistic concurrency control and software transactional memory (STM) that resolves the common mismatch between databases*

and programming languages. Its unique ability to create and deploy logical multi-site configurations of applications provides unrivaled continuity of business in the face of not just unplanned events, but also planned events, including planned events that include changes to application logic and schema.

Worldwide, GT.M is used in multiple industries, including finance, health care, transportation, manufacturing and others. GT.M supplies the processing power to the FIS Profile™ enterprise banking application.

http://www.fisglobal.com/

GT.M is free and distributed under the GPL license.

1.2.2 InterSystems Caché

From the Intersystems web site:

InterSystems Caché® is an advanced database management system and rapid application development environment. With Caché, you'll make breakthroughs in processing and analyzing complex Big Data, and developing Web and mobile applications. Caché uniquely offers lightning-fast performance, massive scalability, and robust reliability – with minimal maintenance and hardware requirements.

This is a new generation of database technology that provides multiple modes of data access. Data is only described once in a single integrated data dictionary and is instantly available using object access, high-performance SQL, and powerful multidimensional access – all of which can simultaneously access the same data.

Caché comes with several built-in scripting languages, and is compatible with the most popular development tools.

http://www.intersystems.com/

As of this writing, Intersystems distributes a free, single user personal copy at their web site.

1.2.3 An Open Source Implementation by Ray Newman

From the web site:

Implementation of ANSI Standard MUMPS 1995 and ISO/IEC 11756 for FreeBSD, OSX and linux. Also on the Raspberry Pi (ARM) under debian and Windows under cygwin. This is the post-relational database.

http://sourceforge.net/projects/mumps/

This is a free distribution.

1.2.4 GPL Mumps

GPL Mumps is a free, open source implementation written by Kevin O'Kane, with the assistance of students, for Linux, BSD and Cygwin. The source code download is available at:

http://www.cs.uni.edu/~okane/

Although this distribution was designed mainly for Linux, it will run in Microsoft Windows with certain restrictions and qualifications. The examples in this book were developed using GPL Mumps.

The GPL Mumps implementation adds to the Mumps definition support for specialized text processing and scientific applications. Some of these extensions are shown in the text below but the full documentation is at the link given above.

In the examples below, the reader will note that most programs begin with the line:

```
#!/usr/bin/mumps
```

For a file of Mumps source code, this line invokes the GPL Mumps interpreter in Linux, Unix or BSD based operating systems. Following system conventions, it provides the the name and location of the interpreter that will execute program in the file. You should not include this line if you are using another implementation.

2 Data Types

Mumps variables are not typed. The basic data type is string although integer, floating point and logical (true/false) operations can be performed on string variables.

The values in a string are normally any ASCII code between 32 to 127 (decimal) inclusive although some systems allow for an extended character set range including the ASCII control codes (1 through 31) as well as other character sets. For portability, the standard specifies that strings not be longer than 255 characters but most implementations permit strings considerably longer than this.

String constants are enclosed in double quote marks ("). A double quote mark itself can be embedded in a string by placing two immediately adjacent double quote marks ("") in the string.

The single quote mark (') is the *not* operator with no special meaning within quoted strings. The convention used in some programming languages to precede special characters such as the single quote mark by a backslash character does not apply in Mumps.

A constant consisting of a numeric value (optionally with a plus or minus sign, and a decimal point), need not be enclosed by quotes although doing so has no effect.

The examples in Figure 2 give several valid Mumps character string constants:

```
1    "The seas divide and many a tide"
2    "123.45"
3    123.45
4    "Bridget O'Shaunessey? You're not making that up?"
5    """The time has come,"" the walrus said."
```
                     Figure 2 Example Strings

Note that the two versions of the value 123.45 are equivalent. Also, note the embedded double quote marks in the final example.

The Mumps standard specified that numbers should be able to maintain fifteen significant digits with a range of values over $+/-10^{+25}$ to 10^{-25}. The standard also allowed for numbers to be specified using scientific notation (*e.g.* 6.0221415E+23). Some implementations, however, support numbers with larger ranges.

Mumps has some peculiar ways of handling strings when they participate in numeric calculations.

If a string begins with a number but ends with trailing non-numeric characters, and it is used as an operand in an arithmetic operation, only the leading numeric portion will participate in the operation. The trailing non-numeric portion will be ignored.

On the other hand, if a string beginning with non-numeric characters is used with an arithmetic operand, the string's value will be interpreted as 0. Figure 3 gives several examples.

```
1    1+2           will be evaluated as 3.
2    "ABC"+2       will be evaluated as 2.
3    "1AB"+2       will be evaluated as 3.
4    "AA1"+2       will be evaluated as 2.
5    "1"+"2"       will be evaluated as 3.
6    ""            will be evaluated as 0.
```

Figure 3 String Arithmetic

Logical values in Mumps are special cases. A numeric value of zero, any string beginning with a non-numeric character, or a string of length zero is interpreted as *false*. Any *numeric* string value other than zero is interpreted as *true*.

Logical expressions yield either zero (for *false*) or one (for *true*). The result of any numeric expression can be used as a logical operand. Figure 4 gives several examples.

```
1     "1"                    true
2     "0"                    false
3     ""                     false
4     "A"                    false
5     "99"                   true
6     "1A"                   true
7     "000"                  false
8     "-000"                 false
9     "+000"                 false
10    "0001"                 true
```

Figure 4 Truth Values of Strings

2.1 Variables

A Mumps variable name must begin with a letter or percent sign (%) and may be followed by either letters, the percent sign, or numbers. Variable names are case sensitive. The underscore (_) and dollar sign ($) characters are not legal in variable names.

In Mumps there are no data declaration statements. Variables are created when a value is assigned for the first time to a variable name by either a **set** or **read** command. They may also be created by the **new** command. Once created, variables normally persist until (1) the program ends, (2) they are destroyed by a **kill** command, or (3) the block in which they were created by a **new** command ends. Ordinarily, variables, once created, are known to all invoked routines.

One variation on the above concerns variables received as parameters to routines. These parameter variables are temporary in the invoked routine and destroyed upon exit. However, if a routine calls another routine, all variables known to the calling routine, including parameter variables, are known to the called routine.

Another variation, as noted above, concerns variables that are the result of a **new** command. A **new** command creates a new copy of one or more variables in a subroutine or block and causes any previous values to be pushed down. Upon exit from the block or subroutine containing the **new** command, the **new** versions are destroyed and the previous instances of variables with the same names, if any, are restored.

Local variables, those stored in volatile memory, are limited by the standard to an aggregate size of 10K characters. Most systems, however, permit much larger local storage limits but you should check your vendor's guide. GPL Mumps permits the local variable table to grow to available memory size.

2.2 Arrays

Arrays in Mumps come in two varieties: *local* and *global*. Both, except where noted, have the following characteristics:

- Arrays are not declared or pre-dimensioned.
- A name used as an array name may also, at the same time, be used as the name of a scalar or a label.
- Array elements are created by assignment (**set)** or appearance in a **read** statement.
- The indices of an array are specified as a parenthesized, comma separated list of numbers or strings.
- Arrays are sparse. That is, if you create an element of an array, let us say element 10, it does not mean that Mumps has created any other elements. In other words, it does not imply that there exist elements 1 through 9. You must explicitly create these it you want them.
- Array indices may be positive or negative numbers or character strings or a combination of both.
- Arrays in Mumps may have multiple dimensions limited by the maximum line length (at least 512 bytes).
- Arrays may be viewed as either arrays or trees.
- When viewed as trees, each successive index is part of the path description from the root of the array to a node.
- Data may be stored at any or all nodes along the path of a tree or not at all.
- Global array names are prefixed with the up-arrow character (^) while local arrays are not.
- Local arrays are destroyed when the program ends while global arrays, being disk resident, persist.

For example, consider an array reference of the form *^root("p2","GPL Mumps","d2")*. This could be interpreted to represent a cell in the three dimensional matrix named *^root* indexed by the values *("p2","GPL Mumps","d2")* or, alternatively, it could be interpreted as a path from the origin *(^root)* to a final third level node *d2*.

In either interpretation, values may be stored not only at the end node, but also at intermediate nodes. That is, data values may be stored at nodes *^root, ^root("p2"), ^root("p2","GPL Mumps")* as well as *^root("p2","GPL Mumps","d2")*. Alternatively, no data needs to be stored. The path description isself is the data.

Because Mumps arrays can have many dimensions (limited by system line length), when viewed as trees, they can be of many levels of depth. When viewed as matrices, they cna be of many dimensions.

In Mumps, arrays can be accessed immediately if you know a valid set of indices. Alternatively, you can explore a global array tree by means of the builtin functions *$data()* and *$order()* functions.

The first of these, *$data()*, indicates if a node exists, if it has data, and if it has descendants. The second, *$order()*, is used to navigate from one sibling node to the next (or prior) at a given level of a tree.

2.3 Local Arrays

In Mumps, local arrays are stored in memory. Their contents are lost when the program that creates them terminates. Since local arrays may have string indices and are stored in a run-time symbol table, access to each involves a lookup. This is not as efficient as arrays in traditional languages such as C/C++ and FORTRAN. Figure 5 gives some examples of local array usage (some lines in the following may be wrapped on some readers).

```
1   #!/usr/bin/mumps
2       set a(1,2,3)="text value"
3       set a("text string")=100
4       set i="testing"
5       set a(i)=1001
6       set a("Iowa","Black Hawk County","Cedar Falls")="UNI"
7       set a("Iowa","Black Hawk County",Waterloo)="John Deere"
```

Figure 5 Local Arrays

2.4 Global Arrays

Global arrays are stored on disk. They may be viewed either as sparse multi-dimensional matrices or as tree structured hierarchies. As is the case with local arrays, indices may be a combination of either numeric or text values.

Syntactically, global arrays differ from local arrays only in that global array names are prefixed by an up-arrow character (^). For example, consider the global array named *root* in Figure 6.

In Figure 6, each successive index leads to a new, deeper node in the tree. Some references go deeper than others. Some nodes have data stored at them (not shown in the figure), some have no data. The *$data()* function, described in detail below, can be used to determine if a node has data and if it has descendants.

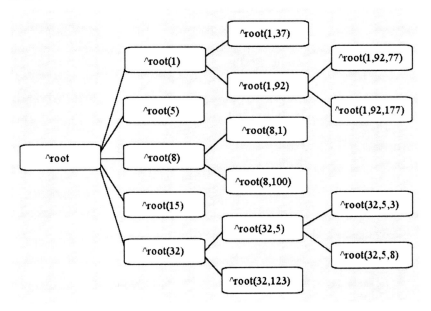

Figure 6 Global Array Tree

In the example in Figure 6, only numeric indices were used to conserve space. In fact, the indices of global arrays are very often character strings.

```
1    #!/usr/bin/mumps
2        set ^root(1,37)=1
3        set ^root(1,92,77)=2
4        set ^root(1,92,177)=3
5        set ^root(5)=4
6        set ^root(8,1)=5
7        set ^root(8,100)=6
8        set ^root(15)=7
9        set ^root(32,5)=8
10       set ^root(32,5,3)=9
11       set ^root(32,5,8)=10
12       set ^root(32,123)=11
```

Figure 7 Global Arrays

In a global array tree, siblings are organized alphabetically. That is, the index with the lowest overall collating sequence value is first and the index with the highest value is last. The *$order()*

function, described below, can be used to navigate from one sibling to the next (or prior) at any given level of the tree. The tree from Figure 6 can be created with the code shown in Figure 7.

In the example in Figure 6 note that several nodes exist but have no data stored at them. For example, the nodes *^root(1)*, *^root(8)* and *^root(32)* exist because they have descendants but they have no data stored. On the other hand, the node *^root(32,5)* exists, has data but also has descendants.

In some cases, an empty string (nothing) is stored at a leaf node of a global array because the path description itself is the actual data. For example, consider the global array containing clinical laboratory tests seen in Figure 8.

In this case, the first index is a patient id number, the second is the name of a lab test, the third is the date of the test and the fourth is the test result. In actuality, no further information is needed: the indices contain all the data. The *$data()* and *$order()* functions (see below), can be used to extract the values from what, in this case, is more a four column table than a tree.

A more realistic example can be seen in the Figure 10 which shows a section of the Medical Subject Headings (MeSH) as developed by the U.S. National Library of Medicine.

```
1    #!/usr/bin/mumps
2       set ^lab(1234,"hct","05/10/2008",38)=""
3       set ^lab(1234,"hct","05/12/2008",42)=""
4       set ^lab(1234,"hct","05/15/2008",35)=""
5       set ^lab(1234,"hct","05/19/2008",41)=""
```

Figure 8 Global Array with Null Data

In Figure 10, a sub-tree of the National Library of Medicine MeSH hierarchy is represented along with the corresponding Mumps code to create the sub-tree.

Quote marks around the numeric indices are not required except in cases where you want to preserve leading zeros as is the case in some nodes.

As noted above, data may be stored not only at fully subscripted terminal tree elements but also at other levels. For example, a three dimensional matrix named *mat1*, could be initialized as shown in Figure 9. In this example, all the elements of a traditionally structured three dimensional matrix of 100 rows, 100 columns and 100 planes are initialized to zero. Note: the **for** command is the iterative loop command in Mumps. Its arguments are a loop variable, an initial value, an increment, and a final value. This matrix is similar to the C matrix shown in Figure 11 although the Mumps matrix can store data values other than **ints**.

```
1  #!/usr/bin/mumps
2    for i=0:1:100 do
3    . for j=0:1:100 do
4    .. for k=0:1:100 do
5    ... set ^mat1(i,j,k)=0
```

Figure 9 Global Data Only at Leaf Nodes

However, unlike other programming languages there are other nodes of the matrix which could have been initialized such as indicated by the example in Figure 12.

In effect, this means that *mat1* can also be a single dimensional vector, a two dimensional matrix and a three dimensional matrix simultaneously. This is not possible in traditional languages.

Furthermore, not all elements of a matrix need exist. That is, the matrix can be sparse as is shown in Figure 13.

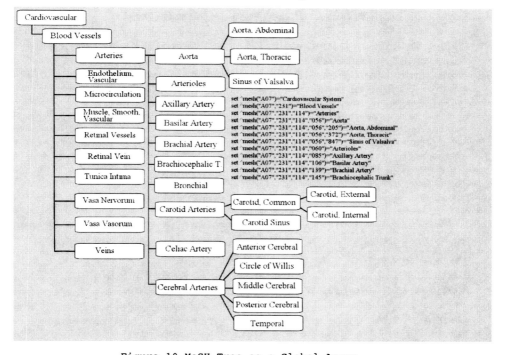

Figure 10 MeSH Tree as a Global Array

```
1  int mat1[100][100][100],i,j,k;
2  for (i=0, i<101; i++)
3          for (j=0; j<101; j++)
4                  for (k=0; k<101; k++)
5                          mat[i][j][k]=0
```

Figure 11 C Matrix

In the example in Figure 13, only index values 0, 10, 20, 30, 40, 50, 60, 70, 80, and 90 are used to create each of the dimensions of the array and, consequently, only those elements of the matrix are created. The omitted elements do not exist. This also is not possible in traditional languages.

While global arrays are unique to Mumps, as a programmer, you will work with them as though they were ordinary arrays but the system interprets them as path descriptions in the system's external data files.

Global arrays may have both string and numeric indices as shown in Figure 14.

```
1   #!/usr/bin/mumps
2      for i=0:1:100 do
3      . set ^mat(i)=i
4      . for j=0:1:100 do
5      .. set ^mat(i,j)=j
6      .. for k=0:1:100 do
7      ... set ^mat1(i,j,k)=k
```

Figure 12 Global Data at Several Levels

The Mumps global array facility had its origin in the early use of Mumps for medical databases which are often viewed as hierarchical in nature. The Mumps global arrays were a solution to the problem of how to represent the tree-like structure of patient data in a simple and easily manipulated structure.

```
1   #!/usr/bin/mumps
2      for i=0:10:100 do
3      . for j=0:10:100 do
4      .. for k=0:10:100 do
5      ... set ^mat1(i,j,k)=0
```

Figure 13 Sparse Global Array

By way of example, consider the simplified patient record shown Figure 15. At the top level is the patient's id node at which is stored the patient's name. At the second level, are nodes for demographic information (such as address, gender, phone number, *etc*.) and a link node node for clinical data.

```
1    #!/usr/bin/mumps
2       set a="1ST FLEET"
3       set b="BOSTON"
4       set c="FLAG"
5       set ^ship(a,b,c)="CONSTITUTION"
6       set ^captain(^ship(a,b,c))="JONES"
7       set ^home(^captain(^ship(a,b,c)))="PORTSMOUTH"
8       write ^ship(a,b,c)  → CONSTITUTION
9       write ^captain("CONSTITUTION")  → JONES
10      write ^home("JONES")  → PORTSMOUTH
11      write ^home(^captain("CONSTITUTION"))  → PORTSMOUTH
12      write ^home(^captain(^ship(a,b,c)))  → PORTSMOUTH
```

Figure 14 Global Array Indices

Clinical data is often organized by diagnostic or problem category and each problem or diagnostic code is divided into episodes of the problem organized by onset date. For a given problem and onset, the data are divided by category (medications, lab tests, orders, notes, *etc.*) which are further subdivided by, in the case of lab tests, test name, date, time and result.

In the code example below, the tree is named *patient*. The Mumps code to populate the tree might look like the example in Figure 15.

The first index of the tree is the patient's SSN or other id number. At the second level is a code number indicating is lower levels contain address information, lab data, and so forth. The codes are shown as Mumps variables but the values stored in the tree are the numbers associated with each variable.

```
1    #!/usr/bin/mumps
2        set ssn="123-45-6789"
3        set addr=1
4        set strt=2
5        set cty=3
6        set st=4
7        set zip=5
8        set dx=6
9        set lab=7
10
11       set ^patient(ssn)="Jones, John, J"
12       set ^patient(ssn,addr,strt)="123 Elm St"
13       set ^patient(ssn,addr,cty)="Anytown"
14       set ^patient(ssn,addr,st)="IA"
15       set ^patient(ssn,addr,zip)="50613"
16
17       set icda="789.00"
18       set date="6/23/2008"
19       set ^patient(ssn,dx,icda,date)="Dr Smith"
20
21       set test="HCT"
22       set time="10:45"
23       set rslt=45.2
24
25       set ^patient(ssn,dx,icda,date,lab,test,time,rslt)=""
26
27       set time="18:45"
28       set rslt=42.3
29
30       set ^patient(ssn,dx,icda,date,lab,time,rslt)=""
```

Figure 15 Global Array Examples

Notice at the last line that the empty string is stored at the node. In this cases, the actual data (the lab test result) is the actual value of the final index.

Also, note that each intermediate node need not be explicitly created nor contain data: the nodes representing lab, dx, lab, and so forth are not separately created. Their creation is implicit in constructing the longer paths of which they are intermediates.

In Mumps, the database is part of the language which has caused some to ask if it is a database with a language or a language with a database? A bit of both, actually.

2.4.1 Naked Global References

A *naked* global reference is a throwback to the early days of Mumps when Global arrays were stored internally as multi-way trees (most are now stored in B-trees). In order to reduce the file processing overhead, the system kept track of the point of the last global array reference. A naked reference was a global array reference would proceed from the last reference as starting point rather than from the origin or root of the entire global array tree structure. This was done to save time on the early file systems before B-trees had been invented.

Thus, if a previous global array reference was:

```
^a(1,2,3,4)
```

A subsequent reference of the form:

```
^(5,6)
```

would be the same as saying:

```
^a(1,2,3,5,6)
```

That is, the first subscript of the naked reference becomes the last subscript of the most recent reference.

The naked indicator is, in almost all cases, set to be the last reference to a global array. This reference may have been set in another program than the one currently running. Thus, from a code analysis point of view, it is impossible, when looking at an arbitrary naked reference, to be completely certain of what it actually references.

Needless to say, naked references are a bad programming idea but they are widely and confusingly used in some programming packages. GPL Mumps does not support naked references.

2.5 Environments

Some Mumps implementations also define environments which collect and localize Mumps routines and global arrays in order to implement security restrictions. Consult your user's guide for specific details.

2.6 Collating Sequences

Commercial Mumps implementations may support other character sets and collating sequences than ASCII. In these, array indices may be presented in numeric order rather than character order. See your implementation guide for details.

3 The Basics

Mumps was originally conceived as a language to be executed by interpreters. Consequently, the basic syntax and structure of the commands tend to be line oriented and simple to parse.

Each command (Mumps refers to statements as *commands*) in Mumps begins with a keyword. The keyword may be abbreviated, in many cases to a single letter (this was to save storage and time in the interpreter). In most cases, a command may be optionally followed by a *post-conditional* expression and then, in most cases by one or more arguments.

A post-conditional, discussed in detail below, is an expression immediately following a command word. If the expression is true, the command is executed. If the expression is false, the command is skipped and execution advances to the next command.

The following is an example of a post-conditional applied to the **set** command (**set** assigns a value to the variable specified on the left hand side of the equals sign):

```
set:a=b  i=2
```

The **set** command will execute the assignment if variables *a* and *b* are equal. A post-conditional begins with a colon and is followed by an expression which is evaluated to be either true or false.

Mumps programs are not free format. Blanks are significant. Many people programming in Mumps for the first time have problems because they elect to ignore the rules about placement of blanks. Blanks are terminators in Mumps. They are used to separate a command keyword from its arguments and to terminate a list of arguments.

In general, these are the syntax rules:

- A line may begin with a label. If so, the label must begin in column one.

- After a label there must be at least one blank or a *<tab>* character before the first command.

- If there is no label, column one must be a blank, a *<tab>*, or a semi-colon followed by some number of blanks, possibly zero. If the character in column one is a semi-colon (;), the remainder of the line is a comment. If not, a command is expected.

- After most command words, or abbreviations of same, there may be an optional post-conditional. The post-conditional begins with a colon and consists of an expression which will be evaluated and interpreted as *true* or *false*. The command does not execute if the expression is *false*. No blanks or *<tab>* characters are permitted between the command word and the post-conditional.

- If a command has an argument, there must be at least one blank after the command word and its post-conditional, if present, and the command's argument.

- Expressions (both in arguments and post-conditionals) may *not* contain embedded blanks except within double-quoted strings.

- If a command has no argument and it is the final command on a line, it is followed by the new line character.

- If a command has no argument and is not the final command on a line, there must be at least two blanks after the command (and any attached post-conditional), before the next line item.

- If a command has an argument and it is the final command on a line, its last argument is followed by a new line character.

- If a command has an argument and it is not the last command on a line, it is followed by at least one blank before the next command word or semi-colon.

- A semi-colon causes the remainder of the line to be interpreted as a comment. The semi-colon may be in column one or anywhere a command word or abbreviation is permitted.

- Command words, functions and builtin variables are normally case insensitive while the case of variable names is case sensitive (check you implementation).

3.1 Mumps Expression Precedence

Expressions in Mumps are evaluated strictly left-to right *without* precedence. If you want a different order of evaluation, you **must** use parentheses to indicate same. This is true in any Mumps expression in any Mumps command and is a common source of error, especially in **if** commands with compound predicates.

For Example:

    a<10&b>20

really means

    (((a<10)&b)>20)

when you probably wanted

$$(a<10)\&(b>20)$$

3.2 Mumps Commands

Mumps is a line oriented command language. Each line of code contains one or more commands and most commands have one or more arguments separated from one another by commas that are evaluated and executed from left to right.

For example, the assignment command is **set** and the following shows an iunstance with three operands:

```
set a=10,b=a*2,c=b*2
```

In the example, 10 is assigned to variable *a*, 20 is assigned to variable *b* and 40 is assigned to variable *c*.

The full list of Mumps commands is given in Figure 16 although some implementations may have added to this set.

break	implementation defined
close	release an I/O device
database	set global array database (GPL Mumps only)
do	execute a program, section of code or block
else	conditional execution based on $test
for	iterative execution of a line or block
goto	transfer of control to a label or program
halt	terminate execution
hang	delay execution for a specified period of time
if	conditional execution of remainder of line
job	create an independent process
lock	access/release a named resource
kill	delete a local or global variable
merge	copy arrays
new	create new copies of local variables
open	obtain ownership of a device
quit	end a for loop or exit a block

read	read from a device
set	assign a value to a global or local variable
tcommit	commit a transaction
trestart	roll back / restart a transaction
trollback	roll back a transaction
tstart	begin a transaction
use	select which device to read/write
view	implementation defined
write	write to device
xecute	dynamically execute strings
z...	implementation defined – all begin with the letter z

Figure 16 Table of Mumps Commands

3.3 Creating and Assigning Values to Variables

Variables in Mumps, as noted above, can be local, that is, present only during the execution of the program, or global, which is to say, disk resident and persistent after the program terminates. Both local and global variables may be either scalars or arrays although most local variables tend to be scalar and most global variables tend to be arrays in practice.

A variable, either global or local, is created by appearing on the right hand side of a **set** command, as an argument in a **read** statement or by the **new** command. Both **read** and **set** initialize a new variable or alter an existing variable. The **new** command creates an uninitialized (empty) variable.

The Mumps symbol table is dynamic and variables are created as needed. They may also be explicitly destroyed by the **kill** command or, in the case of variables that are subroutine parameters or created in by the **new** command, as a result of exiting a subroutine or block.

Mumps expressions may involve both local and global variables, operators and constants. Constants may be either numeric or string. String constants are enclosed in double quotes (use two immediately adjacent double quotes to embed a double quote within a quoted string). Strings are converted to numerics as needed and back again. The basic internal data type is string.

The assignment command is the **set** command as shown in the examples in Figure 17. The expression to the right of the equals sign is evaluated and assigned to the variable on the left hand side.

1	`#!/usr/bin/mumps`	`; interpreter`
2	`set i=2 write i`	`; writes 2`
3	`set i=2*3 write i`	`; writes 6`
4	`set i="2"*3 write i`	`; writes 6`
5	`set i="  2"*3 write i`	`; writes 6`
6	`set i="""hello""" write i`	`; writes "hello"`
7	`set ^a="test" write ^a`	`; writes test`
8	`set a="test" write a`	`; writes test`
9	`set ^a(1)="test" write ^a(1)`	`; writes test`
10	`set a(1)="test" write a(1)`	`; writes test`

Figure 17 Expressions

3.4 Scope of Variables

In Mumps, variables once created are normally known throughout your program and any routines your program invokes until either the program ends or you explicitly **kill** it.

Thus, if your program invokes a code segment, either from disk or in another part of the currently loaded routine (using the **do** or **goto** commands), the invoked segment has full access to all variables in existence at the time of the invocation.

Likewise, if an invoked routine creates or modifies variables by means of the **set** or **read** commands and then returns to the invoking routine, these variables are available to the invoking routine with the values they acquired in the invoked routine.

However there are exceptions to this rule and these involve variables passed as parameters or variables created by the **new** command.

A variable created by the **new** command will be freed upon exit from the code block in which it was created. A code block is defined as a body of code entered as a result of a **do** command.

When a **new** command creates a variable and there already is a variable with the same name, the pre-existing variable is *pushed down* and a new instance of a variable with the same name becomes the visible. When the variable created by the **new** command is freed, the old variable *pops up* and becomes visible again. Examples are given in the section on the **do** command below.

Another exception to the normal scope rule concerns variables passed as parameters to a routine invoked by a **do**. In the called routine, formal parameters (that is, those received by the routine) are local to the routine and any routines called by it. If a variable of the same name as a formal parameter exists in the symbol table, it is *pushed down* in the same manner as with the **new** command. Upon exit from the called routine, the variables represented by the formal parameters are freed and any previous versions of variables with the same names are *popped up* again. Examples are given in the section on the **do** command below.

4 Overview of Commands and Concepts

We begin with a quick introduction to a few basic commands and concepts. More detailed analysis will come later.

4.1 The Set Command

The **set** command is used to assign the results of calculations to variables. It may have multiple arguments, separated by commas, which will be executed from left to right.

Each argument consists of a reference to a variable or a function, an equals sign (=), and an expression. The result of the evaluation of the expression on the left hand side of the equals sign is assigned to the variable or function on the right hand side. For example:

```
set a=2*3
set b(5)=$len("abcd")
set ^c(123)=b(5)
set x="aaa.bbb.ccc"
set $piece(x,".",2)="xxx"
set i=0,j=0,j=0
```

In the first, the result of the arithmetic expression, 6, is assigned to the variable *a*. The variable is created if it does not already exist.

In the second, the value 4 is assigned to the array element *b(5)*. The element is created if it does not exist. The *$len()* function returns an integer giving the length of the argument passed to it.

In the third example, the element of the global array *^c(123)* is assigned 4 (the value in *b(5)*). The global array element is created if it did not exist.

The fourth line initializes the variable *x* with a string.

In the fifth line we see a function (*$piece()*) being used on the right hand side of the equals sign. The function is discussed in detail below (see section 9.13). The function receives the value *xxx* from the left hand side and substitutes it for the second piece of the variable *x*. The result in variable *x* is *aaa.xxx.ccc*.

In the final example we see a **set** command with three arguments. They are executed from left to right.

4.1.1 Operators

There are a large number of operators in Mumps. These include the usual +, -, * *and* / (add, subtract, multiply and divide) as well as many others some of which are peculiar to Mumps. These are discussed in detail in Chapter 5 below.

4.2 Input/Output

Input/output in Mumps involves reading and writing strings to the current input or output object. Most formatting of output and parsing of input takes place in functions that process the strings before output or after input.

The object from to which data will be read or written is determined by a command named **use** to be discussed later. By default, until the program changes it, input is from *stdin* (usually your console keyboard) and output is to *stdout* (usually your console screen). Note: *stdin* and *stdout* can be redirected.

4.2.1 I/O Format Control Codes

Both the input/output commands **read** and **write** may use formatting codes. The formatting codes in Mumps are very simple and the full set is and shown in Figure 18.

!	new line (!! means two new lines, *etc.*)
#	new page
?x	advance to column "x" (newline if needed)

Figure 18 **Read/Write** Format Codes

These codes are embedded in commands as operands and are executed, reading left to right. For example:

```
write "The time has come",!,?5,"The walrus said",!
```

writes the first string on one line, skips to the next, indents to column 5, then writes the second string then skips to the beginning of the next line.

4.2.2 The Read Command

The **read** command reads input from the current I/O unit (determined by the **use** command). By default, it reads from *stdin* (usually your keyboard).

Typically, the operands to the **read** command are the names of scalar or array, local or global variables. For example:

```
read a,b(99),^c(i,j,k)
```

For each operand, the command will attempt to read a line and place its contents, minus the new line character, into the next variable. In this mode, only full lines are read.

If the **read** command is reading from your keyboard (that is, *stdin* has not been re-directed), the command may contain output formatting codes as well as string constants in addition to the variable names to be read. This permits prompts to be embedded in the **read**. For example:

```
read !,"Enter name:",?20,x
```

This writes a new line, followed by the prompt "Enter name:" and then the cursor tabs to column 20 and awaits the user input which will be stored in variable x.

Prompts may be used only when I/O is directed at a console keyboard/screen combination.

A full discussion of **read** is found in section 6.17 below.

4.2.3 The Write Command

The **write** command executes format codes and writes strings to the current output object (be default, *stdout*).

Since internally, Mumps variables are stored as strings, no format codes are needed to convert from an internal binary format to printable characters.

The **write** command has one or more operands. These are either formatting codes as discussed above, variables or the the string results of expressions.

The embedded white space format control codes, shown above, cause a new line (!), new page (#) or tabbing to a specific column (?). In the case of the tab operation, a number or a numeric valued expression follows the question mark. If the current cursor position is beyond the desired column, a new line is started and the cursor moves to the designated column.

Numbers may be formatted by means of functions such as *$justify()* and *$fumber()*. Some examples of the **write** command can be found in Figure 19.

A full discussion of **write** is found in section 6.25 below.

1	`#!/usr/bin/mumps`	Invokes Mumps interpreter.
2	`write "hello world",!`	Writes text and new line.
3	`set i="hello",j="world" write i," ",j,!`	Writes contents of i, a blank, contents of j, and a new line.
4	`set i="hello",j="world" write i,!,j,!`	Writes contents of i, skips to a new line, writes contents of j and skips to a new line.
5	`write 1,?10,2,?20,3,?30,4,!`	Writes 1, skips to column 10, writes 2, skips to column 20 ...

Figure 19 **Write** Examples

4.3 The If Command

The argumented form of the **if** command tests one or more expressions for *true* and does or does not execute the remainder of the line depending upon the result.

The **if** command has as its scope *only* the remainder of the line on which it appears.

If the expression or expressions in the arguments to the **if** are *false*, the *entire* remainder of the line is ignored. This is different than in most other programming languages.

If an argument to an **if** evaluates to a value of zero, a string beginning with a non-numeric character, or a string of length zero, the argument is interpreted to be *false*. All other non-zero numeric results are interpreted as true. For example:

```
if 0 write "zero" ; false no write
if 1 write "one" ; true - writes
if (10/2)=(15/3) write "yes" ; true - writes
if 1,2,3 write "123" ; true - writes
if 1,0,3 write "103" ; false - no write
```

If there are multiple arguments to an **if** (a comma separated list), the arguments are evaluated left to write. If an argument is true, evaluation continues with the next argument. If an argument is false, evaluation ends and execution resumes on the next line of the program.

All arguments must be *true* in order for the remainder of the line following the **if** to be executed. In effect, the arguments in a multiple argument **if** command are *and'ed* together.

Execution of an **if** command has the side effect of setting a system built-in variable known as *$test*. If all the arguments to an **if** command are *true*, *$test* is set to *true* (1), *false* (0) otherwise. In addition to **if**, *$test* is also set by several other commands.

Note: since the **if** command has scope of the remainder of the line on which it appears, the **else** command should normally *not* appear on the same line. The **else** executes only when *$test* is *false*. **else** is not really part of the **if**. It can be, and is, used as a standalone command whose effect is based solely upon *$test*.

An example of such a situation would be where a command on the same line as the **if** might itself alter **$test** and the **else** is used to initiate an action if based on that reset. For example:

```
if a>b set a=10 else   set a=20
```

In the above, the first **set** command is executed if *a>b*. The second **set** command is not executed since *$test* is true and the remainder of the line following **else** is discarded.

However, if *a>b* is false, the remainder of the line following the **if**, including the **else** command and the code following it, is not executed.

The argumentless form of the **if** command (in which the **if** is followed by two or more blanks) tests the current value of *$test* and executes the remainder of the line if *$test* is *true* (1). For example, see Figure 20.

```
1    #!/usr/bin/mumps
2      set i=1
3      if i=1 write "yes",!
4      if  write "yes again",!
```

Figure 20 If Without Arguments

The code segment in Figure 20 will write "yes" and "yes again" because the first **if** sets *$test* to *true* and the second *if* executes as well because *$test* is still *true* when line 3 is executed.

A negative side effect of this is that *$test* can be reset to *false* in the scope of the first **if** as can be seen in Figure 21 which will only write *yes*. The second **if** on line 2 sets *$test* to *false* and thus the **if** on line 3 does not execute the remainder of its line.

```
1    #!/usr/bin/mumps
2      set i=2
3      if i>1 write "yes",! if i>2 write "yes yes",!
4      if  write "yes again",!
```

Figure 21 $Test With Argumentless If

4.3.1 Logical Operators

In Mumps the *and* operator is the ampersand (**&**), the *or* operator is the exclamation mark (**!**) and the *not* operator is the single quote mark(**'**) and they have the same meanings as in other programming languages. For example:

```
set a=1,b=0
a&b is false
a!b is true
a&('b) is true
```

4.3.2 Relational Operators

The relational operators given in Figure 22. A full discussion of each of these is given below but Figure 23 has a few examples.

Note the two arguments on line 5 in Figure 23. The comma effectively constitutes an *and* operation since, if the first argument is *false*, processing of the command halts. Both arguments must be true for the remainder of the line to be executed.

Also, note line 6 in Figure 23. Due to strict left-to-right, non-precedence parse, the expression is interpreted as though it had been written:

```
(((i<j)&k)>j)
```

=	equals
'=	not equals
>	greater than
<	less than
'>	not greater than (less than or equal)
'<	not less than (greater than or equal)
[	contains
'[	not contains
]	follows
']	not follows

Figure 22 Relational Operators

Here, the sub-expression *i<j* is *true* (1). The result is then *and'ed* with *k: 1&k* which results in *true* (1) however, this result (1) is now compared with *j: 1>j*, which is *false* so the entire expression is *false*. The expression on line 7 is probably what was intended. Bottom line: it is very important to include parentheses in compound expressions to express precedence.

```
1    #!/usr/bin/mumps
2        set i=1,j=2,k=3
3        if i=1 write "yes",!              ; yes
4        if i<j write "yes",!              ; yes
5        if i<j,k>j write "yes",!          ; yes
6        if i<j&k>j write "yes",!          ; does not write
7        if i<j&(k>j) write "yes",!        ; yes
8        if i write "yes",!                ; yes
9        if 'i write "yes",!               ; does not write
10       if '(i=0) write "yes",!           ; yes
11       if i=0!(j=2) write "yes",!        ; yes
```

Figure 23 Using Relational Operators

4.4 Blocks

Originally, all Mumps commands had only line scope. That is, no command extended its influence beyond the line on which it appeared. As a result, some line of Mumps code were very long and complicated. In later years, however, a limited block structure facility was added to the language.

In Mumps, blocks are entered by the argumentless form of the **do** command (thus requiring two blanks between it and the next command, if any). The lines following a **do** command belong to the **do** if they begin with an incremented level of dots. The block ends when the number of dots declines to an earlier level.

This can be seen in Figure 24 which will write *a is 1*. If the variable *a* has the value 1 the **do** command executes causing the block defined by the single level of dots to execute. Otherwise, the

do is not executed and execution resumes at the line following line 4. The single dot preceding the command on these lines indicates a block at indent level one.

Blocks can be used to create code that looks more familiar to programmers rather than the long, run-on **if** statements often associated with early Mumps programs.

```
1    #!/usr/bin/mumps
2       set a=1
3       if a=1  do
4       . write "a is 1",!
```

Figure 24 Blocks

This can be seen in Figure 25. Note the two spaces after the **else** on line 6. In this example, only one block will be entered depending on the value of *a*.

```
1    #/usr/bin/mumps
2       set a=1
3       if a=1  do
4       . write "a is 1",!
5       . set a=a*3
6       else   do
7       . write "a is not 1",!
8       . set a=a*4
9       write "a is ",a,!
```

Figure 25 Blocks with **If** and **Else**

Blocks can be nested as shown in Figure 26 which illustrates two levels of blocking. The outer block, consists of those lines beginning with one dot. This block is dependent on the first **if** command.

The inner blocks, consisting of the lines beginning with two dots, are dependent on the **if** and **else** commands, respectively.

```
1    #!/usr/bin/mumps
2       set a=1,b=2
3       if a=1  do
4       . set a=0
5       . if b=2  do
6       .. set b=0
7       . else   do
8       .. set b=10
9       . write b,!
```

Figure 26 Multi-level Blocks

In the case of blocks, *$test* is *restored* to its previous value upon normal exit from a block as shown in Figure 27. Here, *$test* becomes *true* with the first **if** command and the block following it is entered. Inside the block *$test* becomes *false* because of the second **if** command. However, upon exiting the block, *$test* reverts to its previous value, *true*, and, consequently, *987* is not written. Note: in GPL Mumps if a block is exited by a **goto**, *$test* is not restored and retains its last value. It is an error to exit a block with a **goto** in standard Mumps.

```
1   #!/usr/bin/mumps
2       set i=1
3       if i=1 do
4       . if i=0 write 123,!
5       else   write 987,!
```

Figure 27 $Test with Blocks

However, in single line scope *if* commands, *$test* is not restored at the end of a line as shown in Figure 28. In this case, *$test* first becomes *true* on line 3 and then, due to the second **if**, *false*. Consequently, the **else** command on line 4 *is* executed and *987* is written. *$test* reverts to its original value only upon normal exit from a block.

```
1   #!/usr/bin/mumps
2       set i=1,j=2
3       if i=1 if j=0 write 123,!
4       else   write 987,!
```

Figure 28 $Test without Blocks

A **quit** command causes a block to be exited but execution will continue on the line containing the invoking **do** command.

Implementations may place an upper limit on the number of nested blocks.

4.5 The For Command

The iterative command in Mumps is **for**. It has several variant forms. In the most common form, a local variable (globals not permitted) is initialized and either incremented or decremented by a specified amount until some limit value is achieved.

In a second form, a local variable is initialized and incremented or decremented by a specified amount but there is no upper or lower limit.

In a third form, a local variable is assigned values from a specified list of values.

In a fourth form, no local variable or list of values is used (two blanks follow the command), and the **for** becomes an *iterate forever* command.

Examples of the first form of the **for**, incrementing or decrementing a variable until some limit is reached, can be seen in Figure 29.

In the first example on line 2, *i* is initialized to 1 (the value after the equals sign), incremented by 1 (the value after the first colon), until it becomes 10 (the final value). The **write** command executes ten times writing the values one through ten.

In the second example on line 3, *i* is initialized to 10 and decremented by 1 until it reaches 0. The **write** displays the numbers 10 through 0.

In the example on line 4, the increment is 2.

```
1    #!/usr/bin/mumps
2       for i=1:1:10 write i,!     ; 1,2,...9,10
3       for i=10:-1:0 write i,!    ; 10,9,...2,1,0
        for i=1:2:10 write i,!     ; 1,3,5,...9
```

Figure 29 **For** Command Examples

For loops may be nested as shown in Figure 30.

```
for i=1:1:10 write !,i,": " for j=1:1:5 write j," "

output:

1: 1 2 3 4 5
2: 1 2 3 4 5
3: 1 2 3 4 5
.
.
.
10: 1 2 3 4 5
```

Figure 30 Nested **For** Loops

If the upper limit is omitted, the loop becomes infinite:

```
for i=1:1 write i,! ; writes 1,2,...9,10,...
```

In the case where no upper limit is specified, some form of loop termination is obviously desirable. That's the job of the quit command. The quit command exits the nearest for loop. In the following, the quit is only executed when the post-conditional becomes true:

```
for i=1:1:10 write i,! quit:i>5 ; writes 1,2,3,4,5,6
```

Because for has as its scope the remainder of the line it is on, a post-conditionalized quit is often used to terminate a for rather than an if and a quit because an if (which also has line scope) would own the remainder of the line.

A comma list of values may be used:

```
for i=1,3,22,99 write i,! ; writes 1,3,22,99
```

Both modes may be mixed:

```
for i=3,22,99:1:110 write i,! ; writes 3,22,99,100,...110

for i=3,22,99:1 write i,! ; writes 3,22,99,100,101 ...
```

Finally, with no arguments, the command becomes *do forever* (until the **quit** executes).

```
; the following writes 1,2,3,4,5
set i=1
for  write i,! set i=1+1 quit:i>5
```

Note the two blanks following the **for** command. These are required as the **for** has no arguments.

In this context of the **for**, the **do** command can be useful as shown in Figure 31.

```
1   #!/usr/bin/mumps
2      set i=1
3      for  do  quit:i>5
4      . write i,!
5      . set i=i+1
```

Figure 31 Quit with Block Example

In Figure 31, the **for** iterates forever. The **do** executes the block that follows the **for** (lines 4 and 5).

Upon return from the block, the **quit** command will execute if *i* is greater than five.

If the **quit** is not executed, the **for** re-iterates. Otherwise, when the **quit** is executed, the **for** terminates and execution continues at the first statement following the block.

In the context of a block, the **quit** command means to quit the block, not the **for** as shown in Figure 32 or, in a nested environment as shown in Figure 33.

```
1  #!/usr/bin/mumps
2     for i=1:1:10 do
3     . write i
4     . if i>5 write ! quit
5     . write " ",i*i,!

   output:

   1 1
   2 4
   3 9
   4 16
   5 25
   6
   7
   8
   9
   10
```

Figure 32 Quit in an Iterative Block

Note: if the **quit** in Figure 33 were in the innermost block, it would only end that block - not the **for**. The governing **for** would re-iterate. Thus, the **quit** needs to be on the same line as the **for** command in order to terminate the **for**. In this example, the final **write** command executes after the inner nested loop has terminated. It provides the new-line character (!).

```
1    #!/usr/bin/mumps
2      for i=1:1:10 do
3      . write i,": "
4      . for j=1:1 do   quit:j>5
5      .. write j," "
6      . write !

output:

1:  1 2 3 4 5 6
2:  1 2 3 4 5 6
3:  1 2 3 4 5 6
.
.
.
8:  1 2 3 4 5 6
9:  1 2 3 4 5 6
10: 1 2 3 4 5 6
```

Figure 33 **Quit** in a Nested Block

4.6 Input/Output Units

For input/output, Mumps uses a scheme based on a unit number or a device, depending on implementation. Consult your user's guide. In this text, only unit numbers are used.

When a **read** or **write** command is executed, input or output is read or written to the device or file associated with the currently designated I/O device. Unit numbers or devices become associated with files and I/O options by the **open** command and designation as to which is the current unit or device is done by the **use** command.

The unit number currently active is in the system builtin variable **$io**.

By default, programs begin with **$io** having a value of 5 (this may vary, depending upon implementation). Unit 5 is system's the console screen and keyboard (*stdin* and *stdout* in Linux terminology).

While unit number 5 is permanently associated with *stdin/stdout,* you may associate unused unit numbers with devices or files with the **open** command and disassociate from same with the **close** command.

As with most languages, you should **close** files that you have used for output as this will insure that all the buffers have been written to the device.

When you execute a **read** or **write** command, the system reads or writes to the unit whose number is in the system builtin variable **$io**.

The **use** command sets **$io** to one of the available I/O units. This designation remains in effect until changed.

For example, the Mumps program in Figure 34 copies the contents of file *aaa.dat* to file *bbb.dat*. File *bbb.dat* is created if it did not previously exist or overwritten if it did.

The **open** command associates files or devices with unit numbers. The details and parameters of the **open** command differ greatly from one vendor to another and are implementation defined. The example in Figure 34 uses GPL Mumps syntax.

```
1    #!/usr/bin/mumps
2        open 1:"aaa.dat,old"
3        if '$test write "error on aaa.dat",! halt
4        open 2:"bbb.dat,new"
5        if '$test write "error on bbb.dat",! halt
6        write "copying ...",!
7        set f=0
8        for  do  quit:f
9        . use 1
10       . read rec
11       . if '$test set f=1 quit
12       . use 2
13       . write rec,!
14       close 1,2
15       use 5
16       write "done",!
```

Figure 34 **Open** and **Close** Commands

```
1    #!/usr/bin/mumps
2        set in="aaa.dat,old"
3        set out="bbb.dat,new"
4        open 1:in
5        if '$test write "error on ",in,! halt
6        open 2:out
7        if '$test write "error on ",out,! halt
8        write "copying ...",!
9        set f=0
10       for  do  quit:f
11       . use 1
12       . read rec
13       . if '$test set f=1 quit
14       . use 2
15       . write rec,!
16       close 1,2
17       use 5
18       write "done",!
```

Figure 35 **Open** Command

In the program in Figure 34, unit numbers become associated with files on lines 2 and 4. In this syntax, the unit number, a constant, is placed before the colon. In the string or string expression following the colon, the file name is specified (this may contain directory information).

In GPL Mumps, after the file name, you include a comma followed by either *new, old,* or *append* depending upon if the file is being created (or re-created) for output, an existing file is being opened for input or and existing file is being opened for output with new material being added at the end. Device parameters are system specific. Consult your user's guide for details on your implementation.

If the **open** succeeds, *$test* is *true, false* otherwise (note the expression '$test in the Figure 34 means "not *$test."*

Also, each **read** command sets *$test* to *true* if it is successful. On end of file, *$test* is set to *false* and the loop terminates.

The argument to the **open** following the colon may be a variable as shown in Figure 35.

4.7 Post-Conditionals

Generally speaking, as noted above, a post-conditional is an expression that is evaluated prior to executing the arguments of a command. The exceptions are the **do** and **goto** commands where post-conditionals may be applied both to the command and individual arguments.

In all commands, if the post-conditional expression attached to the command word is false, all the arguments of the command are not executed and control moves to the next command. In the **do** and **goto** commands, if the command level post-conditional is true, and if the arguments are post-conditionalized, the argument level post conditionals are evaluated. Examples:

```
set x=10
set:x<100 i=99 ; arg executed
write:x>1 "hello" ; arg not executed
do:x<100 lab1:x<90,lab2:x<10 ; lab1 entered, lab2 not
```

Some commands, such as the **if** and the **else**, may not be post-conditionalized.

Figure 36 shows some valid commands with and without post-conditionals.

The reason for post-conditionals is rooted in the original single line scope of Mumps programs. For example, if you have a single line **for** loop but need to include conditional execution of a command in the body of the loop, an **if** command would cause the remainder of the line to be ignored should the expression in the **if** command be *false.*

For example:

```
for i=1:1:20 if i<10 set ^a(i)=^b(i) else ^a(i)=^c(i)
```

The above will not work as planned. For values of *i* less than ten, the assignment from *^b(i)* to *^a(i)* will take place and the **else** clause not executed.

However, when *i* is ten or larger, the remainder of the line following the **if** command is ignored and the **else** is likewise not executed. This is because the *then* clause of the **if** has scope of the remainder of the line on which it appears and thus the **else** is not executable in this context.

```
1    #!/usr/bin/mumps
2
3      set i="hello world"
4
5      set i="hello",j="world"
6
7    ; Post-conditionalized set command. The single
8    ; argument (i="hello world") is only executed
9    ; if "a=10" is true:
10
11     set:a=10 i="hello world"
12
13   ; A normal goto:
14
15     goto label1
16
17   ; A post-conditionalized goto. Only executed if "a<b"
18   ; is true:
19
20     goto:b<a label1
21
22   ; A goto with a post-conditionalized argument.
23   ; Branch taken only if "c>d":
24
25     goto label1:c>d
26
27   ; Multiple argument level post-conditionals. Branch
28   ; taken on first true expression:
29
30     goto lab1:c>d,lab2:d<e
31
32   ; A post-conditionalized quit. Note that quit takes
33   ; no arguments and thus has two blanks following
34   ; its post-conditional:
35
36     quit:a=b  set i="hello"
37
38   ; Example of post-conditional at the command and
39   ; argument level. None of the arguments are evaluated
40   ; if "a=10" not true:
41
42     goto:a=10 lab1:c>d,lab2:d<e
```

Figure 36 Post-conditionals

To solve this problem, post-conditionals were introduced. The above can be fixed with the following:

```
for i=1:1:20 set:i<10 ^a(i)=^b(i) set:i'<10 ^a(i)=^c(i)
```

The first **set** is executed only when *i* is less than ten and the second **set** executed only if *i* is greater than or equal (not less than) ten.

Alternatively, with the introduction of blocks, the above would now more properly be written as is shown in Figure 37. (Note the two blanks following the **else** as it has no arguments.)

```
1     #!/usr/bin/mumps
2        for i=1:1:20 do
3        . if i<10 set ^a(i)=^b(i)
4        . else   set ^a(i)=^c(i)
```

Figure 37 Using **If/Else** in Loops

4.8 Navigating Arrays

Global (and local) arrays are navigated by means of the *$data()* and *$order()* functions. The first of these determines whether a node exists, if it has data and if it has descendants. The second permits you to move from one sibling to another at a given level of a global array tree.

The function *$data()* returns a zero if the array reference passed to it as a parameter does not exist. It returns one if the node exists but has no descendants, ten if it exists, has no data but has descendants and eleven if it exists, has data and has descendants.

The second function, *$order()*, returns the next ascending (or descending) value of the last index of the array reference passed to it as an argument.

You pass *$order()* an array reference. It evaluates the last index of the reference and returns to you the next ascending or descending value of the last index or an empty string if there are no more values.

By default, indices are presented in ascending collating sequence order unless you specify a second argument of -1. In this case, the indices are presented in descending collating sequence order.

To find the lowest (first) or highest (last) value of the index, you use the empty string as the last index of the reference passed to *$order().*

For example, if you have a global array named *abc* with indices 1 through 9 inclusive, *$order()* yields the following:

```
$order(^abc("")) returns 1
$order(^abc(""),-1) returns 9
$order(^abc(5)) returns 6
$oders(^abc(5),-1) returns 4
```

In GPL Mumps, numeric indices are returned by *$order()* are in ASCII collating sequence order.

For example, if an array has an index with values *"AAA"*, *"1"*, *"2"*, … *"10"*, *"aaa"*, The function *$order()* will return the indices in the order *"1"*, *"10"*, *"2"*, *"3"* … *"9"*, *"AAA"*, *"aaa"*.

```
1    #!/usr/bin/mumps
2       kill ^a
3       for i=1:1:9 s ^a(i)=1
4
5       write $data(^a(1))      ; writes 1
6       write $order(^a(""))    ; writes 1
7       write $order(^a(1))     ; writes 2
8       write $order(^a(9))     ; writes the empty string
9
10      set i=5
11      for j=1:1:5 set ^a(i,j)=j
12
13      write $data(^a(5))      ; writes 11
14      write $data(^a(5,1))    ; writes 1
15      write $data(^a(5,15))   ; writes 0
16      write $order(^a(5,""))  ; writes 1
17      write $order(^a(5,2))   ; writes 3
18
19   ; the following writes 1 through 5
20
21      set j=""
22      for  set j=$order(^a(5,j)) quit:j="" write j,!
23
24      set i="",f=0
25      for  do  quit:f
26      . set i=$order(^a(i))
27      . if i="" set f=1 quit
28      . write i,!
29      . set f1=0
30      . if $data(^a(i))>1 set j=""  for  do  quit:f1
31      .. set j=$order(^a(i,j))
32      .. if j="" set f1=1 quit
33      .. write ?5,j,!

     lines 24 through 32 write:
     1
     2
     3
     4
     5
             1
             2
             3
             4
             5
     6
     7
     8
     9
```

Figure 38 Navigating Global Arrays

Other vendors may present numbered values in numeric order prior to alphabetic values, depending on the implementation defined collating sequence settings. You should consult your implementation's user manual. Figure 38 gives some examples of *$order()* and *$data()*.

4.9 Command line parameters

In most implementations command line parameters may be passed directly to a Mumps program. The details of how this is done will depend upon your operating system and the specific implementation. The Mumps Standard did not deal with this issue.

In GPL Mumps, command line parameters can be accessed as shown in Figure 39. The parameters, by convention, will be found in the Mumps variables named: *%0, %1, %2, ...* and so forth upon program startup. The variable *%0* will always be present and will be the name of the program being run.

If using the interpreter, *%0* will be */usr/bin/mumps* and *%1* will give the name of the file being interpreted. The variables *%2, %3, ...* will contain the values of the command line parameters. Thus, in the interpreter, the actual command line parameters begin with *%2*.

In the case of compiled programs, *%0* will be the name of the compiled executable and variables *%1, %2* and so forth, they will contain the values of the command line parameters. You can check if these exist with *$data()*.

```
    $ ./cc.mps 111 222 aaa bbb

1   #!/usr/bin/mumps
2     write %0,!,%1,!
3     set f=0
4     for i=2:1 do  quit:f
5     . if '$data(@("%"_i)) set f=1 quit
6     . write @("%"_i),!

    writes:

    /usr/bin/mumps
    ./cc.mps
    111
    222
    aaa
    bbb
```

Figure 39 Command Line Parameters

4.10 Indirection

Indirection is one of the more powerful and also dangerous features of the language. With indirection, strings created by your program, read in from a device, or loaded from a database can be evaluated and executed at runtime.

Indirection occurs at two levels. One is by means of the unary indirection operator (@) which causes the string value to its right to be executed as code. The other is by means of the **xecute** command which executes its string expression argument as command level text. Figure 40 gives several examples.

As shown in Figure 40, string expressions, whether created in the program or read in (line 11) can be executed as code. String operators can also be used to construct global array references (line 9), reference external routines (line 12) and as a complete command argument (line 13).

The other form of indirection occurs at the command level. In this form, the result of the **xecute** command, the commands to be executed are essentially unknown until actual execution as seen in Figure 41.

The **xecute** command can be used to execute one or more commands contained in a string. On line 2, of Figure 41, the contents of the variable a are interpreted and executed as ordinary code. Line 3 is a more extensive example incorporating the indirection operator as well. The example of line 7 reads (infinite loop) strings from the input unit and executes them.

1	`set a=123`	
2	`set b="a"`	
3	`write @b,!`	`writes 123`
4	`set c="b"`	
5	`write @@c`	`writes 123`
6	`set d="@@c+@@c"`	
7	`write @d`	`writes 246`
8	`write @"a+a"`	`writes 246`
9	`set @("^a("_a_")")=789`	
10	`write ^a(123)`	`writes 789`
11	`read x write @x`	`who knows?`
12	`set a="^m1.mps" do @a`	`execute ^m1.mps`
13	`set a=",b=123" set @a`	`assign 123 to b`

Figure 40 Operator Indirection

1	`set a="set b=123+2 write b"`	
2	`xecute a`	`; 125 is written`
3	`set a="set b=""c"" set c=""1+1"" write @@b"`	
4	`xecute a`	`; 2 is written`
5	`set b="a"`	
6	`xecute @b`	`; 2 is written`

Figure 41 Command Indirection

From a software engineering point of view, indirection is fraught with problems but from a programming point of view, it is a very powerful tool. It should be used with caution, however.

4.11 Subroutines and Parameter Passing

4.11.1 Subroutines Invoked by Do or Goto

The concept of subroutines evolved during the history of Mumps. In the earliest versions, small segments of code, either in the current routine or in a disk resident routine, could be invoked by means of the **do** or **goto** commands.

When a segment of code is invoked by the **do** command, return is normally made to the point in the line next following the invoking argument.

In the case of code segments invoked by the **goto** command, on the other hand, no return is made.

The **do** command is thus the main means of invoking what might be considered subroutines. Originally, there was no means to pass parameters to an invoked segment. However the entire Mumps local symbol table was visible to any code segment invoked and any changes made to variables in invoked code were known upon return.

In the original design, segments of code executed by **do** commands were not isolated from the invoking program. Instead, there were merely extensions of the active program. Consequently, *$test* was not restored to its original value upon return from a segment of code invoked by a **do** command.

The original specification defined two ways to invoke a segment of code. In one form, the argument of the **do** command is a local label in the current routine or, optionally, a local label followed by a plus sign and a numeric offset (negative offsets are not permitted).

When this form of **do** is executed, transfer of control is made to the line containing the label. If an offset is present, execution begins at line *label+n* where *n* is the value of the offset. Lines of code are executed until a **quit** is encountered or end of file (considered equivalent to a **quit**) is reached. At that time return is made to invoking line of code. (Note: When used with the **do** command, offsets must be preceded by a label (this is not the case with the *$text()* function.)

The other way to specify code to be executed by the **do** command is similar. However, instead of a label, the argument to the **do** is the name of a file, usually on disk, containing Mumps source code. The file name is preceded by a circumflex to distinguish it from a local label. In this form, the designated file is loaded, executed and return is ultimately made to the invoking line of code in the original routine.

The file name format may also include a label and an offset. In this case, the file name is preceded by a label followed, optionally, by a plus sign and and offset. This combined format is used to specify an entry point other than the first line of the file.

In all cases, return to the invoking routine takes place on end of file or a **quit**.

In later language standards this concept was extended to include parameter lists for both the **do** and **job** commands (**job** starts a concurrently running child process).

Parameter lists are parenthesized comma separated of one or more constants, expressions or variables. They immediately follow the label or the file name if one is present. A label must always be present. In the case where a label and a file name are provided, the file will be loaded and execution will begin at the label given. Labels used with pass parameter lists may not be followed by offsets as above.

Parameters that are constants, the result of expression evaluation, or global array references are always passed to the invoked code by value (in call by value - a copy of the parameter is passed). Changes in the called code to a call-by-value parameter variable have no effect on the corresponding original variable in the calling routine.

Local variables, however, from the calling routine may be passed either by value or by reference (call by reference). Changes in the called routine to these variables change the originals in the calling routine.

Variables may be omitted from the calling program's parameter list but there must be a comma to indicate their omission except where the omitted variable(s) are at the end of the list. The corresponding variables in the called routine will be undefined.

In the invoked program code (which may be in the currently resident code segment or in a file to be loaded), there must be a label with the same name as the label in the **do** command.

If parameters are to be passed, the label in the invoked code must be followed by a parenthesized list of variables to receive the parameters. These will be assigned positionally with the first passed parameter assigned to the first receiving variable and so on. The receiving list must be contain at least as many variables as the calling parameter list. If receiving list contains more variables, those variables not assigned values will be undefined in the called program.

In the case of call by value, the variable in the invoked code receiving the value is local and temporary. It is destroyed upon return to the calling program. The corresponding variable in the calling program is unchanged.

Variables in the symbol table are available to the called program and may be modified. However, if a variable with the same name as the variable receiving a value in the parameter list already exists in the symbol table, the variable in the symbol table is protected: it is *pushed down* during execution of the invoked code, and restored upon return.

When a variable is passed by reference, changes to the variable in the called code segment are reflected in the original variable. That is, changing the variable in the invoked code changes the corresponding parameter variable in the calling program. As in the case with call-by-value variables, if a variable already exists in the calling program with the same name as the parameter in the called routine, it is likewise *pushed down* and subsequently restored.

Variables are passed by reference by having have their names in the calling program's parameter list preceded by a period (decimal point). However, no period is placed in front of the corresponding variable name in the invoked code. Call by reference is not permitted for the **job** command.

Figure 42 gives some examples of several alternatives.

The example on line 1 invokes a segment of code at label *lab1* in the currently resident routine. Return is made to the point immediately following the label.

The example in line 2 invokes the code segment at label *lab1* and, upon return, the segment at label *lab2*.

In line 3, the file *file1.mps* is loaded, executed from the beginning and return is made to line 3.

In line 4, file *file1.mps* is loaded and execution begins at the line with the label *lab3*.

```
1    do lab1
2    do lab1,lab2
3    do ^file1.mps
4    do lab3^file1.mps
5    do lab3+4^file1.mps
6    do lab2(a,b,c)
7    do lab4^file2.mps(a,b,c)
8    do lab3(.a,.b,c)
9    do lab5^file3.mps(.a,.b,c)
```

Figure 42 **Do** Command Examples

Line 5 is the same as line 4 except execution begins 4 lines after the line with the *lab3* label.

Lines 6 and 7 show passing parameters by value. In Line 6, the invoked code is in the currently resident routine and in line 7, in a file named *file2.mps*. In both cases, at the corresponding labels in the invoked code, there must be a parenthesized list of at least three variable names.

Lines 8 and 9 show two parameters being passed by reference (*a* and *b*) and one (*c*) by value.

4.11.2 Extrinsic Functions and Extrinsic Variables

Extrinsic variables are function references without parameters while extrinsic functions are functions that have parameters.

Extrinsic functions and variables return results from the execution of external blocks of Mumps code. They were added in later editions of the Mumps standard. An extrinsic is identified by the presence of two dollar signs (*$$*) preceding the code reference. When invoked, the external (disk resident) code block is executed and the result, by means of a required argumented **quit** command, is returned to the invoking program.

Figure 43 gives some simple examples. The figure shows three disk resident files.

The first file, named *s6.mps*, is shown in lines 1 through 8. The second, named *s6a.mps*, in lines 9 through 12 and the third, named *s6b.mps*, in lines 13 through 16.

```
1    #!/usr/bin/mumps
2    ; s6.mps
3        set %=$$^s6a.mps
4        write "expect 6 ",%,!
5
6        set p=4
7        set %=xx^s6b.mps(p)
8        write "expect 16 ",%,!
9
10
11   #!/usr/bin/mumps
12   ;   s6a.mps
13       set a=1,b=2,c=3
14       quit a+b+c
15
16   #!/usr/bin/mumps
17   ;   s6b.mps
18   xx(k)    set k=k*k
19            quit k
20
```

Figure 43 Extrinsics

First, the main function, *s6.mps*, invokes the extrinsic *variable* *s6a.mps*. The result calculated by *s6a.mps* is returned on line 12 and this, in *s6.mps* becomes the value of % on line 3. *S6a.mps* is an extrinsic variable because is receives no parameters. It does, however, have access to the data base, the run time symbol table and other system resources such as files.

On line 7 of *s6.mps* the extrinsic *function s6b.mps* is invoked and it is passed the parameter *p*. The entry point *xx* must be given because one or more parameters are being passed. The result is returned on line 16 and becomes the value of % on line 7. *S6b.mps* is a function because it receives parameters.

In addition to passing parameters by value, as shown, *call by reference* is also possible for extrinsic functions just as is the case with routines invokes with the **do** command.

If a parameter is passed in the calling routine with the variable name preceded by a period (decimal point), the variable is passed by reference and thus any changes to the variable made by the called routine are changes to the variable in the calling routine. Variables in the called routine's parameter list do not have periods before their names.

An additional form for external variables and functions, identified by leading *$&* characters, is used to invoke code packages written in other languages. See your vendor's guide for details. Details about this feature vary by implementation.

5 Mumps Operators

The following is a discussion of the operators used in Mumps. Remember, in a Mumps expression, there is no precedence. Evaluation is strictly left to right except when you insert parentheses.

5.1 Assignment operator (=)

The only assignment operator in Mumps is the equals sign. There is no composite assignment operators as in C/C++, Java, *etc*. Cascading assignment is not permitted. Thus the command:

```
set a=b=c
```

exemplifies two meanings of the equal sign: the rightmost is interpreted as the equality comparison operator and the leftmost is the assignment operator. Consequently either 0 or 1 will be assigned to the variable *a,* not the contents of *c.*

5.2 Arithmetic unary operators: (+, -)

The arithmetic unary operators are: **+** and **-**. The unary plus operator (**+**) has no effect other than to force the expression to its right to be interpreted as numeric and thus be stripped of leading blanks, zeros and any trailing non-numerics. The minus operator also forces numeric interpretation but then negates the result as seen in Figure 44.

```
1    #!/usr/bin/mumps
2      set i="0123 Elm Street"
3      write +i      ; writes 123
4      write -i      ; writes -123
```

Figure 44 Example Unary Operators

5.3 Arithmetic binary operators: (+, -, *, /, \, #, **)

The addition (+), subtraction (-), multiplication (*), and exponentiation (**) are binary operators perform in the same manner as in most programming languages. Operands may be either expressions, constants, variables or array (global or local) references. Operands are given a numeric interpretation (leading blanks, zeros, and trailing non-numeric characters are ignored).

Mumps has two division operators: full division (/) and integer division (\). Full division yields results which may have fractional parts while integer division truncates the answer to an integer. The precision of the results of the full division operator will vary by implementation but will usually be at least the equivalent of double precision floating point.

The modulo operator (#) results in the left operand, modulo the right operand (the remainder). Figure 45 has several examples.

5.4 Arithmetic relational operators: (>, <, '>, '<)

The greater than (>) and less than (<) relational operators compare *numbers*. If the operands are not numbers, they are given a numeric interpretation. The result is either zero for *false* or one for *true* as seen in Figure 46.

1	2+3	yields 5
2	2.31+1	yields 3.31
3	3-5	yields -2
4	7/4	yields 1.75
5	7\4	yields 1
6	11#3	yields 2
7	3**2	yields 9

Figure 45 Binary Arithmetic Operators

1	1>2	yields 0
2	2>1	yields 1
3	1<2	yields 1
4	2<1	yields 0

Figure 46 Relational Operators

Both relational operators may be negated producing not greater than ('>) and not less than ('<) (note: the single quote mark is the negating operator) as seen in Figure 47. There is no *less than or equals* or *greater than or equals* operators as such.

1	1'>2	yields 1
2	2'>1	yields 0
3	1'<2	yields 0
4	2'<1	yields 1

Figure 47 Negated Relationals

5.5 String binary operator: (_)

The only binary string operator is concatenation (_) represented by an underscore character. Figure 48 gives examples.

1	"abc"_"xyz" yields "abcxyz"
2	"abc"_123 yields "abc123"
3	123_456 yields 123456

Figure 48 String Binary Operator

5.6 String relational operators: = [ ] ? '? '= '[']]] ']]

The equals relational operator (= and '=) tests for equality as shown in Figure 49.

1	if "abc"="abc" write "EQUALS"
2	if "abc"'="abc" write "EQUALS"

Figure 49 Equality Relational Operators

In Figure 49, the text "EQUALS" will be written to the terminal in line 1 and not in line 2. The not-equals operator is formed by the single quote mark and the equals sign. The equals and not-equals operators may be used with strings or numbers.

Note: when comparing numerics, minor internal differences between two floating point values, even if they print the same decimal value, may result in inequality.

The contains operators ([and '[) determine if the right hand string operand is contained in the left hand string as shown in Figure 50. The word "YES" will be printed for line 2 and not printed for line 3.

```
1    set A="NOW IS THE TIME"
2    if A["THE" write "YES"
3    if A'["THE" write "YES"
```

Figure 50 Contains Operator

The follows operators (] and ']) determine if the left hand string operand follows the right hand string in the current collating sequence as shown in Figure 51. The word "YES" will not be printed for the first example and will be printed for the second.

```
1    set A="NOW"
2    if A]"THE" write "YES"
3    if A'["THE" write "YES"
```

Figure 51 Follows Operator

The sorts-after operator (]] and ']]) is similar to the follows operator but it is collating sequence dependent. That is, depending upon the collating sequence in use, it may yield a different value than the follows operator. See your implementation guide for further details.

5.7 Pattern match operator

The pattern matching operator (? and '?) is used to determine if a string conforms to a certain pattern.

Pattern matching may vary on your system depending upon the character set in use. In GPL Mumps, it is possible to use regular expressions in addition to the codes shown below. Consult your user's guide.

```
1    A for the entire upper and lower case alphabet.
2    C for the 33 control characters.
3    E for any of the 128 ASCII characters.
4    L for the 26 lower case letters.
5    N for the numerics
6    P for the 33 punctuation characters.
7    U for the 26 upper case characters.
8    A literal string.
```

Figure 52 Pattern Match Codes

Figure 52 gives a list of the native pattern match codes. A pattern code is made up of one or more of these, each preceded by a count specifier. The count specifier indicates how many of the named item must be present. Alternatively, an indefinite specifier - a decimal point - may be used to indicate any count (including zero) as can be seen in Figure 53.

```
1   set A="123-45-6789"
2   if A?3N1"-"2N1"-"4N write "OK"
3   if A'?3N1"-"2N1"-"4N write "OK"
4   set A="JONES, J. L."
5   if A?.A1",".A write "OK"
6   if A'?.A1",".A write "OK"
```

Figure 53 Example Pattern Matching

5.8 Logical operators: &, ! '

The binary logical operators *and* (**&**), *or* (**!**) and *not* (**'**) may be applied in the usual manner. The user should note, however, that since Mumps has strict left-to-right precedence, the results can sometimes be unexpected as noted above. Some examples are shown in Figure 54.

```
1   1&1         yields 1
2   2&1         yields 1
3   1&0         yields 0
4   1&1>1       yields 0
5   1!1         yields 1
6   1!0         yields 1
7   0!0         yields 0
8   2!0         yields 1
```

Figure 54 Logical Operators

The *not* operator may be used in conjunction with other operators to form compound operators. The resulting compound operators are shown in Figure 55.

```
1   '< not less than
2   '> not greater than
3   '= not equal
4   '[ not contains
5   '] not follows
6   '? not pattern
```

Figure 55 Negated Operators

5.9 The indirection operator: @

The indirection operator permits direct execution of expressions contained in strings. That is, if you have a string with a valid Mumps expression in it, the @ operator can be used to execute the expression and returns its result. An example is shown in Figure 56.

Figure 57 gives a more complicated example of indirection with using the *$order()* function and a global array reference. The expression executed by the indirection operator on line 10 is:

```
^x(y)
```

```
1    set a="2+2"
2    write @a,!

output: 4
```

Figure 56 Indirection Example

```
1    #!/usr/bin/mumps
2    kill ^x
3    set ^x(1)=99
4    set ^x(5)=999
5    set v="^x(y)"
6    set y=1
7    set x=$order(@v)
8    write x,!
9    set v1="^x"
10   set x=$order(@(v1_"("_y_")"))
11   write x,!

output:

5
5
```

Figure 57 Indirection with $Order()

6 Commands

Each statement in Mumps begins with a unique command word. Often the command word is abbreviated to one or two characters. There are abbreviations for all commands. Excessive use of abbreviations cam make your code unreadable.

The format of a command normally consists the command word or letter, followed (optionally) by a post-conditional, followed by exactly one blank, followed by the arguments to the command (if any).

Most commands may have multiple arguments which are separated from one another by commas.

If a line is to have more than one command, each command is separated by one or more blanks from the next command except when a command has no arguments in which case at least two blanks are required to separate the commands. Blanks are significant in Mumps.

As noted, most commands may be post-conditionalized. A post-conditional is a logical expression which is used to determine if the command (and some cases, all or some of its arguments) should be executed.

A post-conditional appears as a colon followed by an expression. If the expression evaluates to 0 (*false*), the entire command (or individual argument) is not executed. If the expression evaluates non-zero, the command or argument is executed.

The following are examples of command abbreviations, multiple commands per line and post-conditionals:

```
set i=10*5
```

same as above with command word abbreviation:

```
s i=10*5
```

an assignment command with multiple arguments:

```
set i=10*5,j=5,k=i+j
```

a line with multiple commands:

```
set i=10*5 set j=5 s k=i+j
```

an assignment post-conditionalized assignment command

```
set:i=10 j=0
```

6.1 break (abbreviation: b)

In standard Mumps, **break** had no specific purpose or argument definition. It is often used as a debugging aid to halt the interpreter and permit inspection of variables. Check your implementation's user guide.

In GPL Mumps, the **break** command is used to immediately exit the block currently being executed by a **do** command. It may be post-conditionalized. This usage only applies to blocks. In GPL Mumps, the **break** command may not be used other than in a block.

In GPL Mumps, when a **break** occurs in a block, the block is exited and execution continues on the line following the block. The remainder of the line containing the **do** which invoked the block is not executed. Figure 58 gives an example if a **break** being used to prematurely terminate and outer loop. In this example, the program writes 1 through 6 and the block is exited when *i* becomes 6. Execution continues at line 4. The **for** loop is terminated as a result.

```
1   #!/usr/bin/mumps
2   for i=1:1:10 do
3   . write i,!
4   . if i>5 break
5   write i,!
```

Figure 58 GPL Mumps **Break** Examples

In Figure 59, the program writes 1 and 3. The **do** on line 2 (note the 2 blanks following it) is executed and the block beginning on line 2 is entered. The **write** on line 3 writes 1 and then the block is exited due to the **break** on line 4. The **write** commands on lines 2 and 5 are not executed but the **write** on line 6 is executed. In Figure 60, the numbers 1, 2, 4, and 5 are written.

```
1   #!/usr/bin/mumps
2   do    write 2,!
3   . write 1,!
4   . break
5   . write 4,!
6   write 3,!
```

Figure 59 GPL Mumps **Break** Examples

```
1   #!/usr/bin/mumps
2   do
3   . write 1,!
4   . do
5   .. write 2,!
6   .. break
7   .. write 3,!
8   . write 4,!
9   write 5,!
```

Figure 60 GPL Mumps **Break** Examples

See also **quit**. In GPL Mumps, the main difference between **quit** and **break**, is that a **quit** returns to the line containing the **do** for possible further commands whereas the **break** does not.

6.2 close (abbreviation: c)

The **close** command disconnects from a device in standard Mumps. In GPL Mumps, it closes a unit number and makes the unit number available for other uses. It also frees the system buffers. As I/O varies by implementor, see your implementation guide for details as to how this command works on your system.

The **close** command may be post-conditionalized and it may have multiple arguments. Figure 61 gives some GPL Mumps style examples.

```
1    close 4
2    close:k=j 1,2
3    set i=1 close i
```

Figure 61 **Close** Examples

6.3 do (abbreviation: d)

The **do** command has several forms. It may be used to execute a block of local code (the no argument form), a remote section of code in your currently memory resident program, or a block of code stored in a file on disk. The **do** command may be post-conditionalized and its arguments, if any, may also be individually post-conditionalized.

6.3.1 Do without Arguments (abbreviation: d)

The argumentless **do** causes execution of a local code block. After the block is executed, command is returned to the line containing the **do**.

The line containing the **do** command must immediately precede a block of code to be executed and the block must have a level of dotted indent one greater than that of the line containing the **do**.

A block of code entered as a result of a **do** is terminated by a executing a **quit** or by encountering a line with a lesser level of dotted indent. Both a **quit** and encountering a line with a lesser level of block indent cause a return to the line containing the **do**.

An argumentless **do** must be followed by two blanks unless it is the last command on a line. It may be post-conditionalized.

Figure 62 gives an example. The program writes *123, 345, 999* and then *678*. In this example, the **do** on line 2 causes the block (lines 3 and 4) to be entered. Lines 3 and 4 to be executed. At end of block, return is made to the invoking line (2), and *999* is written, control is then given to line 5 where *678* is written.

The example in Figure 63 writes 123 and 345. In the figure, the block at line 3 is entered as a result of the **do** on line 2 and lines 3 and 4 are executed. Line 5 is not executed because it is not a member of the block and there is no preceding **do** command to enter it.

```
1    #!/usr/bin/mumps
2        do  write 999,!
3        . write 123,!
4        . write 345,!
5        write 678,!
```

Figure 62 **Do** with No Arguments

The argumentless form of the **do** can be used with other statements. For example, note the **if** command shown on line 3 in Figure 64. Here the the program writes 123 then 345. The block consisting of line 4 is entered and executed as a result of the **do** and **if** commands. Upon encountering line 5 with a lower level of indent, control is returned to line 3. As there are no more commands on the line, execution resumes on line 5.

Similarly, in Figure 65, the program writes 345 and 789. The block consisting of line 6 is entered and executed as a result of the **else** and **do** commands.

```
1    #!/usr/bin/mumps
2        do
3        . write 123,!
4        . write 345,!
5        .. write 678
```

Figure 63 **Do** with Multiple Blocks

In Figure 66 the program writes 123 and 789. The block consisting of lines 4 and 5 is entered as a result of the **if** and **do** commands on line 3. Note, however, that the **if** command on line 5 sets *$test* to *false* but that the **do** command on line 6 is not executed. This is because the value of *$test* upon exit from a block is reset to the value it had on entry into the block (in this case to *true* as a result of the **if** on line 3).

```
1    #!/usr/bin/mumps
2        set i=10
3        if i=10 do
4        . write 123,!
5        write 345,!
```

Figure 64 **Do** With **If**

```
1   #!/usr/bin/mumps
2       set i=10
3       if i'=10 do
4       . write 123,!
5       else   do
6       . write 345,!
7       write 789,!
```

Figure 65 **Do** With **Else**

```
1   #!/usr/bin/mumps
2       set i=10,j=20
3       if i=10 do
4       . write 123,!
5       . if j=30 write 456,!
6       else   do
7       . write 345,!
8       write 789,!
```

Figure 66 **Do** Effect on *$Test*

6.3.2 **do** with arguments

6.3.2.1 **do** with a Label Argument

The **do** command with an argument consisting of a label causes the program to branch to the label specified by the argument. Execution continues until a **quit** command is encountered which causes execution to return to the line containing the invoking **do**. If the end of the source code is encountered, it is interpreted as a **quit** command.

The argument label may be local to the current routine or the name and, optionally, a label, in a disk resident Mumps routine.

The **do** command may have multiple arguments in which case each is evaluated sequentially.

Do commands with arguments may be post-conditionalized both at the command and argument level. That is, the **do** command itself and some or all arguments may be followed by a colon and an expression. An argument will be skipped if its post-conditional expression is false. All arguments will be skipped if the command level post-conditional expression is false.

Figure 67 has an example of a label argument to a **do** command that are labels local to the current routine. At the **do** on line 3, execution transfers to the label **www** on line 6. Control is returned to line 3 upon execution of the **quit** on line 7. The program writes *hello world* followed by a newline.

```
1   #!/usr/bin/mumps
2       write "hello "
3       do www
4       write !
```

```
5      halt

6   www   write "world"
           quit
```

Figure 67 **Do** with Label Argument

If *$test* changes in the code executed as a result of a **do** command, the previous value of *$test* is restored when control is returned if the block is exited normally. In GPL Mumps, it is not restored if the block is exited as a result of a **goto**. In standard Mumps, it is illegal to exit a block with a **goto**.

The **do** command may invoke a disk resident program by placing the up-arrow character before the program's file name. This will pause the current program, load the target program, execute it, and return to the point of invocation upon completion. The symbol table is shared between the invoking and called program. That is, variables known to the calling program are also known to the called program. Any changes to variables made by the called program are known to the calling program. Figure 68 has an example.

A label of the form *xxx^yyy* where *xxx* is the label and *^yyy* is the file name, may be used for disk resident routines. Execution of the called program will begin with the label given. Standard Mumps also permits numeric offsets from labels such as *xxx+3^yyy* which means, "being execution at the third line after *yyy*."

```
1    #!/usr/bin/mumps
2        write "hello "
3        do ^pgml.mps
4        write !
5        halt

     where pgml.mps is the following:

     #!/usr/bin/mumps
6        write "world"
7        halt
8
```

Figure 68 **Do** with a File

For example, if the program you want to execute is named */usr/lib/cgi-bin/page.cgi* (a possible server side active web page), it may be addressed as shown in Figure 69.

```
set f="^/usr/lib/cgi-bin/papagena.mps"
do @f
```

Figure 69 **Do** with Indirection

6.3.2.2 do with Label and Parameters

If the argument to a **do** command is a label or file reference, it may be followed by a parenthesized list of arguments. The corresponding label or file function must have a corresponding parenthesized list of variable names to receive the arguments. The arguments from the **do** statement are assigned positionally, one by one, from first to last, to the variables at the target label or program.

Variables named to receive values are temporary variables in the invoked code block. They are created upon entry and exist until a **quit** returns to the invoking **do** command.

If variables of the same name as those in the receiving label exist in symbol table at the time of the invoking **do** command, the pre-existing variables are *pushed down* during execution of the block of code associated with the invoked code. Upon return by a **quit** command, the variables created in the invoked code are destroyed and the original variables of the same name, if any, are restored.

Variables not part of the parameter list that exist at the time of invocation are available to the invoked code. Any modifications to these by the invoked code are retained upon return. However, variables created in the invoked code section are destroyed upon exit.

```
1    #!/usr/bin/mumps
2
3      set a="a1",b="a2"
4
5      write "level 1 start a=",a," b=",b,!
6      do xx("b1","b2")
7      write "level 1 on return a=",a," b=",b,!
8      halt
9
10   xx(a,b)
11     write "level 2 on entry a=",a," b=",b,!
12     do yy("c1","c2")
13     write "level 2 on return a=",a," b=",b,!
14     quit
15
16   yy(a,b)
17     write "level 3 on entry a=",a," b=",b,!
18     quit

     output:

     level 1 start a=a1 b=a2
     level 2 on entry a=b1 b=b2
     level 3 on entry a=c1 b=c2
     level 2 on return a=b1 b=b2
     level 1 on return a=a1 b=a2
```

Figure 70 **Do** with Parameters

In Figure 70, the invocation at line 6 of the block labeled *xx*, at line 10, passes the values "b1" and "b2" as parameters. These become the values of the variables *a* and *b*, respectively in the block beginning on line 10. The old values of *a* and *b* from line 3 are *pushed down*. Line 11 prints the current values of the variables *a* and *b* as "b1" and "b2." Line 12 invokes the block of code labeled *yy*, at line 16, and passes the parameters "c1" and "c2" which become the values for a new set of variables *a* and *b*. The old copies of *a* and *b* are *pushed down*. Line 17 prints the current values of *a* and *b* ("c1" and "c2") and then return is made on line 18.

Upon return to line 12, the values of *a* and *b* in the block beginning at line 16 are destroyed and the previous values, "b1" and "b2," are restored. This is indicated by the printout from line 13. Return is then made by the **quit** on line 14.

Upon return to line 6, the copies of variables *a* and *b* from the block beginning at line 10 are destroyed and the original copies of *a* and *b* are restored as is indicated by the **write** command on line 7.

In addition the the parameters as shown in Figure 70, if you precede a parameter variable in the invoking **do** with a period (decimal point), the variable is *passed by reference* and changes to the variable in the invoked code are reflected in the variable upon return. This is not so for variables passed without the period. These are passed by value. Note: the period only appears in the invoking code.

6.4 else (abbreviation: e)

The **else** command tests the value of the system built-in variable *$test*. If *$test* (abbreviated as *$t*) is *false* (zero), the remainder of the line on which the **else** appears *is* executed. If *$test* is not zero, the remainder of the line is *not* executed. The value of *$test* is set, among other ways, by the **if** statement. Since **else** does not take arguments, it *must* be followed by two blanks.

For example:

```
else  set i=10
```

The **else** does not require a preceding **if** statement. It depends solely on the value of *$test*. See the discussion below on details as to how *$test* may be set.

6.5 for (abbreviation: f)

For is the iterative loop command. It repeats the remainder of the line on which occurs multiple times. The basic command has only single line scope but this may be extended to multiple lines through the **do** command.

The most common basic format is:

```
for var=start:increment:limit
```

In the above, the variable *var* will be initialized to the value of the expression **start** and the remainder of the line will be executed. When the line has finished executing, the variable will be incremented by the value of the expression **increment** and the result tested against **limit**. If the value of **var** exceeds **limit**, execution of the command terminates. If not, the remainder of the line containing the **for** is executed.

If the value is **increment** is negative, the value of **var** decrements and the test against **limit** will result in the command terminating if the value of **var** is less than **limit**.

A **for** command normally terminates when the value of **limit** is reached or exceeded. However, it may be prematurely terminated by the **quit** command on the same line.

If the value of **limit** is omitted, the loop will cycle infinitely until it is terminated by a **quit** command.

If a **for** command has no arguments (and thus, two blanks separate it from the next command), the remainder of the line will iterate infinitely until a **quit** command terminates it.

If, following the equals sign, there is a comma separated list of values, the remainder of the line will iterate with the value of *var* taking on each of the values successively. The values need not be numeric.

```
1    #!/usr/bin/mumps
2
3    ; writes 1 through 10
4         for i=1:1:10 write i,!
5
6    ; writes 10 through 1
7         for i=10:-1:1 write i,!
8
9    ; writes 1,3,5,...9
10        for i=1:2:10 write i,!
11
12   ; writes 1 through 100
13       for i=1:1 write i,! quit:i>100
14
15   ; writes 1 through 100
16       set i=0
17       for  set i=i+1 write i,! quit:i>100
18
19   ; writes 1, 4, 6, ABC and 22
20        for i=1,4,6,"ABC",22 write i,!
21
22   ; writes 2,5,10,11,12 ... 20,30,100,101,...105
23       for i=2,5,10:1:20,30,100:1:105 write i,!
```

Figure 71 **For** Examples

Figure 71 gives basic examples of **for** usage.

If the **for** has no arguments (the "do forever" format), it *must* be followed by two blanks.

6.6 goto (abbreviation: g)

The **goto** command causes unconditional transfer of control. The target may be a local program label or a disk resident Mumps program. Indirection is permitted. Both the command and each argument may be post-conditionalized. In standard Mumps, you may not exit a block with a **goto.**

Permitted argument forms are shown in Figure 72. The first of these causes execution to resume at the local label *abc*. The second causes the current program to terminate and control to be passed to the first executable line in the file named *function*. The third branches to the file named *function* beginning at the label *xxx*. Standard Mumps permits an offset to be added to the label such as:

```
goto xxx+3^function
```

1	goto abc
2	goto ^function
3	goto xxx^function
4	set a="^function" goto @a

Figure 72 **Goto** Arguments

Indirection may be used. if the contents of the variable *lab* are *^function.mps* then the code:

```
goto @lab
```

will branch to the routine *function.mps.* Similarly, the expression following the indirection operator may contain a local label.

6.7 halt (abbreviation: h)

The **halt** command terminates execution of a Mumps program and returns you to the operating system. It may be post-conditionalized. If post-conditionalize, there must be two blanks before the next command. For example:

```
halt:I=3
```

6.8 hang (abbreviation: h)

The **hang** instruction suspends execution of your program for a specified period of time (in seconds). It takes as an argument the number of seconds to wait. It may be post-conditionalized. The hang instruction differs from the halt instruction only in the argument: a hang without an argument is a halt instruction. For example:

```
hang:I=J  2*K
```

6.9 if (abbreviation: i)

The **if** command permits conditional execution. The scope of the command is the remainder of the line unless there is an argumentless **do** command on the line following the **if**.

The **if** command may have multiple arguments separated from one another by commas. These are processed left to right. If one of the arguments to the **if** is *false*, execution proceeds to the next line. All arguments must be *true* for the remainder of the line after the **if** arguments to be executed.

Note that the **else** command in Mumps is not linked to the **if** command. Thus, the **if** line scope can lead to problems:

```
set i=2 if i=3 write "no",! else write "yes",!
```

The **else** can *never* executed.

Expressions are evaluated left to right. This sometimes causes problems for people used to dealing with other languages. For example, the expression:

```
I=0&J<0
```

is always *false* since it is parsed as:

```
((I=0)&J)<0)
```

If *I* is zero, the first expression is *true* (value of 1); if *J* is less than zero, then J is interpreted as *true* giving, as a result of the AND operation (**&**), a value of 1 which is not less than zero - therefore the expression is *false*. On the other hand, if *I* is not zero then, regardless of the value of *J*, the AND operation results in *false* (value of zero) which is not less than zero - therefore *false*. The expression should have been written as:

```
(I=0)&(J<0)
```

The **if** command may be used with no arguments (requires 2 blanks after command word) or with multiple arguments separated by commas. If no arguments are given, the current value of *$test* is examined and, if *true*, the remainder of the line containing the **if** is executed. If multiple arguments are given, each is evaluated. If all are *true*, the remainder of the line is executed. If an argument is not *true*, the remainder of the line including any unevaluated arguments are not executed and execution resumes on the next line.

The **if** command sets *$test*. If all the arguments are *true*, *$test* is set to *true*, *false* otherwise.

Figure 73 gives several **if** examples. An **if** command with single line scope may initially set *$test* to *true*, but a subsequent command on the same line may set it to *false*. Thus, on the next line, *$test* may be *false* even though the expression in the previous **if** was *true* (see example below). Note that *$test* is set *true* by the **if** command in line 7 but to *false* by the failed **open** (file does not exist) on the same line. The **if** on line 8 as a result does not execute.

1	#!/usr/bin/mumps	
2	set i=1,j=2,k=3	
3	if i=1 write "true",!	; writes true
4	if write "true",!	; writes true
5	if i=1,j=2,k=3 write "true",!	; writes true
6	if i=1,j=3,k=3 write "true",!	; does not write true
7	if i=1 open 1:"bad"	; file does not exist
8	if write "222"	; nothing written

Figure 73 **If** Examples

If *$test* is changed in the *then* clause of an **if** command, it is not restored when the clause terminates as shown in Figure 74. In this example, the program writes 1 and 0. *$test* becomes *true* as a result of the first **if** command but *false* as a result of the second **if** command. Thus, at line 4, the value printed for *$test* is false (0).

```
1  #!/usr/bin/mumps
2    set i=22,j=5
3    if i=22 write 1,! if j>10 write 2,!
4    write $test,!
```

Figure 74 **if** With *$test*

In Figure 75, the program writes 1 and 99.

```
1  #!/usr/bin/mumps
2    set i=22,j=5
3    if i=22 write 1,! if j>10 write 2,!
4    else  write 99,!
```

Figure 75 **If** With **Else**

6.10 job (abbreviation: j)

The **job** command creates an independent process. Its argument(s) specify a starting point in the created process either as a reference to a line in the current routine or an external routine and, optionally, with starting line and parameters (see **goto** for examples of how to specify labels and routines). Parameters may be passed but only by value.

A time-out option can be added to the reference (*:timeout*) to determine if the **job** command completed within a specified period of time (in seconds). For the timed version, *$test* indicates if the job completed within the allocated time.

The **job** command may also include vendor specific parameters, consult your implementation guide for further details.

6.11 kill (abbreviation: k)

The **kill** command is used to prune the local symbol table and to delete global arrays.

There are three forms of the **kill** command: the first deletes all entries in the local (i.e., non-global) symbol table; the second deletes specific elements from the local symbol table or specific elements from global arrays; and the third is used to delete all elements from the local symbol table except for certain named symbols. All forms may be post-conditionalized.

The first form - deletes the entire local symbol table - is denoted by the **kill** command alone:

```
kill
```

The second form appears as a list of references (note: indirection is permitted):

```
kill A,B,^G(1,2,33)
```

The above would delete variables *A, B* and the global array node *^G(1,2,33)*. Note: if the global array node *^G(1,2,33)* has descendants, they are also deleted. Also, if a local array node is deleted, any of its descendants are also deleted. If the unindexed name of a local or global array is referenced, the entire local or global array with that name is deleted.

The final form of the **kill** may be used to delete all elements from the local symbol table *except* for certain protected elements listed in the parenthesized argument list. It has the following format:

```
kill (A,B(1,1),K)
```

In the above, the local symbol table will be deleted except for variables *A, B(1,1)* and *K*. All other variables will be lost. Global array nodes may not be used in this form of the **kill** command. Indirection is permitted.

6.12 lock (abbreviation: l)

The **lock** command is used to obtain ownership of system resources, mainly global arrays. The argumentless form releases all currently held locks. The argumented form, with an optional timeout, attempts to gain ownership of the named resources.

In the case of a timeout (*:timeout*), in seconds, *$test* is set to indicate if all the resources were obtained. In the case where there is no timeout, your program waits indefinitely until the resources are obtained.

When a name is specified, for example, a global array reference, ownership is attempted for the node specified and all descendant nodes. If another process attempts to obtain ownership of this or any of the its child nodes, its the attempt will fail.

The **lock** command has several variant forms. In the simple case, where one or more names are specified, the system first releases all locks held by the current process and then attempts to gain ownership of the list of names. Unless a timeout has been specified (colon followed by an expression interpreted as seconds), the lock command will wait until the resources are available.

If more than one name is specified as a parenthesized comma list, the **lock** will not succeed until all names have been obtained.

If a name is preceded by a plus sign (+), the lock is attempted without first releasing other locks. If preceded by a minus sign (-), the lock is released for the named item only.

Obtaining a lock on a resource does not actually prevent other processes from accessing the resource or modifying it. Locks are a signaling mechanism only. Locks do not change the naked indicator.

The **lock** command varies in its implementation by vendor. Consult your vendor's guide for specific details. In many implementations, **lock** has been superseded by the transaction commands **tcommit**, **trestart**, **trollback**, and **tstart**.

6.13 merge (abbreviation: m)

The **merge** command copies an element of an array and all its descendants to another variable.

The command:

```
merge ^a=^b
```

will copy global array ^*b* to global array ^*a* replacing any existing elements of ^*a* that are indexed the same as an element of ^*b*. Other examples are given in Figure 76.

6.14 new (abbreviation: n)

The **new** command is used to create a new, temporary copy of a variable in a block or subroutine. When the block or subroutine ends, the old copy of the variable and its contents are restored. Only scalar (non-array) variables names may be used.

Arguments to the **new** command may be either a comma separated list of variable names or a parenthesized comma separated list of variable names. In the first case, new copies of the variables in the list are created. In the second case, new copies of all known variables except those appearing in the parenthesized list are created. Figure 77 gives several examples.

```
1    #!/usr/bin/mumps
2
3      kill ^a,^b
4
5      set ^a(1)="a"
6      set ^a(1,2)="b"
7      set ^a(1,2,3)="c"
8      set ^a(1,3)="d"
9      set ^b(1)="100"
10     set ^b(1,2)="200"
11     set ^b(1,3)="300"
12
13     merge ^a(1,2)=^b(1)
14
15     set x="^a"
16     set f=0
17     for   do   quit:f
18     . set x=$query(@x)
19     . if x="" set f=1 quit
20     . write x," ",@x,!
21
22     halt

     output:

     ^a("1")  a
     ^a("1","2")  100
     ^a("1","2","2")  200
     ^a("1","2","3")  300
     ^a("1","3")  d
```

Figure 76 **Merge** Examples

In Figure 77, in the block at line 7, a new copy of the variable *a* is created and the old instance is pushed-down. The new value remains in existence and is visible in the second level block beginning at line 10. In line 10 a new variable named *b* is created (no prior version exists). In line 12 the values of *a* and *b* are written.

Upon exiting the inner block, the variable *b* is destroyed. There is no prior version so *b* becomes undefined. This is reflected in line 13 where the value of *$data(b)* is zero indicating that *b* does not exist. The value of *a* is still *99*.

Upon exiting the first level block, the new copy of variable *a* is destroyed and the original copy is now visible again.

The **new** command can also be used to create new copies of variables in subroutines. Upon exit from the subroutine, the new copies are destroyed and any previous copies are restored. The command **new** should only be used in the contest of a block of returnable subroutine.

```
1    #!/usr/bin/mumps
2
3       kill
4
5       set a=123
6       if 1=1 do
7    . new a
8    . set a=99
9    . if 1=1 do
10   .. new b
11   .. set b=102
12   .. write "expect 99 102 ->  ",a," ",b,!
13   . write "expect 99 0 ->   ",a," ",$data(b),!
14
15      write "expect 123 0 ->  ",a," ",$data(b),!
```

Figure 77 **New** Examples

Another way in which variables can be created upon entry to a subroutine and deleted upon exit is via parameter lists. Variable names of received parameters are automatically **new** and are destroyed upon exit from the subroutine.

6.15 open (abbreviation: o)

The **open** command obtains ownership of an I/O resource.

The syntax and semantics of the arguments to **open** vary depending on the resource being opened and Mumps implementation being used. Consult your user guide for full details.

A timeout (*:timeout*) may be specified. The builtin variable *$test* will indicate if the **open** was successful.

In GPL Mumps, the **open** command associates a unit numbers in the range 1 through 4 and 7 through 9 with an external file. Unit 5 is reserved for the user console (*stdin* and *stdout*) and unit 6 is used as a system pipe. After a unit number is opened, it is used during **read** and **write** commands. This is done by means of the **use** command (see below).

As originally used in Mumps, the unit number (either a number or an expression) is followed by a colon and a file name. In GPL Mumps, the file name must be either a variable name or a quoted literal followed by either ",*new*" ",*append*" or ",*old*".

If followed by ",*new*", GPL Mumps assumes you are opening the file for output: any previous files with this name are lost. You may only write to this file. If you open the file with the ",*old*" option, the program assumes the file exists and opens it for input only (reads only). If you specify ",*append*", the file is opened for output with all new data written to the file appearing after the previously existing data. If an error takes place, *$test* is set to zero and the remainder of the command is not inspected. If no error takes place, *$test* will be one. You should not attempt to reference units for which the **open** command returned a *$test* value of 0. Figure 78 gives several examples of **open** in GPL Mumps.

```
1   #!/usr/bin/mumps
2       open 1:"data,old"
3       open 1:"data,new"
4       open 1:"data,append"
5       set x="data,new" open 1:x
6       set x="file1" open 1:x_",new"
7       set x="file1,new" set i=1 open i:x
8       set ^x(1)="file1,new" open 1:^x(1)
9       set x="/home/user/file1,new" open 1:x
```

Figure 78 **Open** Examples

You should be careful to **close** any unit you have opened for output. You must **close** an open unit number before re-using the unit number in another **open** command.

6.16 quit (abbreviation: q)

The **quit** command provides an exit point for a **for**, **xecute** and **do** commands. It may be post-conditionalized. It takes no arguments (therefore, you need two spaces after it if there are any other commands on the same line).

In the case of a single line **for**, a **quit** terminates the nearest **for** loop as seen in Figure 79. In this example, line 2 writes 1 through 6. Line 3 writes 1 through 6 ten times. Line 4 writes 1 through 6 five times.

Pitfall: with a single line **for**, if you use an **if** command to decide whether to **quit**, and if the expression in the **if** is *false*, the remainder of the line is *not* executed. Instead of an **if**, use a post-conditional.

For example, see Figure 80. Line 2 writes nothing because the remainder of the line after the if command is not executed if the expression in the **if** is *false*. When it becomes *true* (when *i* is 6), the **quit** causes termination of the **for**. Thus, the **write** is never reached.

Line 3 writes 1 through 5. The **quit** only executes when *i* becomes 6.

```
1   #!/usr/bin/mumps
2       for i=1:1:10 write i,! quit:i>5
3       for i=1:1:10 for j=1:1:10 write j,! quit:j>5
4       for i=1:1:10 q:i>5   for j=1:1:10 write j,! q:j>5
```

Figure 79 **Quit** Examples

When executed in a block, a **quit** command exits the block and resumes execution of the line containing the **do** command that invoked the block as shown in Figure 81. Here, because the expression is *true* in the **if** command on line 3, the **do** is executed. The **do** causes the block on line 4 to be entered. The **write** command on line 4 writes the number 1. The expression in the **if** command on line 5 is *true* so the **quit** is executed causing control to return to the **write** command on line 3 and which writes the number 4. Consequently, the code in Figure 81 writes the numbers 1, 4 and 3 on separate lines.

```
1   #!/usr/bin/mumps
2       for i=1:1:10 if i>5 quit write i,!
3       for i=1:1:10 quit:i>5 write i,!
```

Figure 80 More **Quit** Examples

The program in Figure 82 writes ten lines each containing a number in the range 1 through 10 followed by the word *End*. The **for** executes the **do** ten times and thus the block writes the current value of *i*. After execution of the block, control returns to line 1 where the word *End* and a new line are written.

```
1   #!/usr/bin/mumps
2       set i=10
3       if i>5 do  write 4,!
4       . write 1,!
5       . if i>9 quit
6       . write 2,!
7       write 3,!
```

Figure 81 **Quit** in a **Do** Block

In the case of a **do** command with arguments, a **quit** returns to the invoking command as seen in Figure 83. Here the program writes 1 and 2. The **do** transfers control to line 5 with the label *sub* where the number 1 is written. The **quit** on line 6 returns control to line 2 and execution then moves to line 3 where the number 2 is written. Note that there is only one blank between the **do** command and the *sub* label on line 2.

```
1   #!/usr/bin/mumps
2       for i=1:1:10 do  write "End",!
3       . write i," "
```

Figure 82 Iterative **Do** Block

```
1   #!/usr/bin/mumps
2     do sub
3     write 2,!
4     halt
5   sub write 1,!
6       quit
```

Figure 83 **Quit** with Remote Block

In Figure 84, the program writes 1 through 5.

When a **quit** is encountered during execution of an **xecute**, execution of the **xecute** text is terminated and control is returned to the original command line.

See also **break**.

```
1   #!/usr/bin/mumps
2       for i=1:1:5 do sub
3       halt
4   sub write i,!
5       quit
```

Figure 84 Iterative Remote Block

6.17 read (abbreviation: **r**)

The **read** command reads data into variables. It may be post-conditionalized. Unless redirected by the **use** command, the **read** command, by default, reads from the user's terminal.

Read command input can be redirected to other devices and files by means of the **use** command (see below). It is a common source of error - sometimes quite destructive errors - for the user to attempt to **read** or **write** to the wrong device. Many Mumps programmers explicitly place the **use** command immediately prior to the **read** or **write** commands to avoid this issue.

Ordinarily, the **read** command takes one or more arguments which may be local scalar variables, local array elements, or global array elements. Each of these is read successively from the input device. When more than one argument is present, a line feed is the delimiter between the successive input values. For example:

```
read A,B,^A(1,3,99)
```

If the input is derived from the user's terminal, the user might type the following sequence in response to the above:

```
22
38
NOW IS THE TIME
```

The **read** command reads one value *per* line.

The **read** command may also write a prompt before it reads. This mode is normally only permitted at the user's console.

The options permitted for "write before read" are: a literal constant in quotes; and a tab, new line, or new page operation. A tab operation is specified by a question mark followed by an expression which is interpreted as arithmetic. The effect is to cause the cursor to move to the named column on the page or screen. The new line operation is caused by typing an exclamation point (!). A new page is induced by the pound-sign (#) character. For example, if you wish to read name, social security number and password with user input from column 20, the following might be appropriate:

```
read "NAME",?20,N,"SSN",?20,S,"PASS",?20,P
```

After the above, the variable *N* will contain the name, *S* the social security number and *P* the password.

The **read** command also permits single character input. That is, a read operation will be satisfied as soon as the user strikes any character on the keyboard: no carriage return is required. The variable will contain a number which is the equivalent of the ASCII character struck. This mode is denoted by preceding the variable to be read by an asterisk. For example:

```
read "ENTER A LETTER ",*A
```

The **read** is satisfied when any character is struck.

There is also another form of the **read**: that which contains "time-outs". Time-outs permit the programmer to specify a maximum interval of time which the program should wait for the user to reply to the **read** operation.

The time-out may be used with either the regular or character by character mode. The time-out is specified by placing a colon after the variable followed by an expression which will be interpreted as numeric. The value of the expression is the number of seconds to wait for a user response to this operation.

If the user fails to respond in the required interval, the *$test* built-in variable is set *false* (0) and the variable contains nothing. If the user does respond in time, *$test* is set *true* (1) and the variable contains the user's reply. For non-character by character mode input, the user must type the carriage return for the input to be valid. If the time-out expires before the user type the carriage return, all input is lost. For example:

```
for  read "ENTER NAME ",name:20 if $test quit
```

In this case the **for** will iterate until the **quit** is executed. Each execution of the **read** will set *$test* depending upon the result of the operation. If a value is typed in for *name* within 20 seconds, *$test* will be *true, false* otherwise. The **quit** is executed when the **read** is successful.

Additionally, if a variable name is followed by a pound (#) sign followed by a numeric expression, the value of the numeric expression limits the number of characters that will be read.

The functions **$piece()** and **$extract()** may be used in the **read** command. In these cases, a section of a string passed as in an argument variable is replaced by the input. For example:

```
set x="123.456.789"
read $piece(x,".",2)
```

If the input is *abc* the string **x** will contain *123.abc.789* after the **read**. Similarly, in the code:

```
set x="123456789"
read $extract(x,4,6)
```

if the input is *abc,* the string **x** will contain *123abc789* after the **read** command.

6.18 set (abbreviation: **s**)

The **set** command is the assignment command for Mumps. The expression on the right hand side of the equals sign is evaluated and placed in the storage associated with the variable on the left hand side. Global variables may be used on the left hand side. The **set** command may be post-conditionalized.

The **$piece** function may be used on the left hand side of an assignment command. For example, if the variable *a* contains the value *aaa.bbb.ccc*, the command:

```
set $piece(a,".",2)="xxx"
```

will result in the value of *a* becoming "aaa.xxx.ccc"

Similarly, The **$extract** function may be used on the left hand side of an assignment command:

```
set x="abcdef"
set $extract(x,3,4)="xx"
```

results in the string "abxxef" in the variable x.

Multiple values may be set at the same time:

```
set (i,^a(1),j,^a(2))=99
```

The above will cause *i, ^a(1), j,* and *^a(2)* to be each set to the value 99.

6.19 tcommit (abbreviation: tc)

The **tcommit** command is part of the transaction processing mechanism. It commits any current pending transactions. See your vendor's guide for specific details. Not available in all implementations.

6.20 trestart (abbreviation: tre)

The **trestart** command rolls back the current transaction and attempts to restart it, depending on the parameters of the originating **tstart** command. If the transaction is not restartable, the command acts as a **trollback** command only. Details are implementation dependent. Not available in all implementations.

6.21 trollback (abbreviation: tro)

The **trollback** command rolls back the current transaction and undoes all changes and locks obtained. Details are implementation dependent. Not available in all implementations.

6.22 tstart (abbreviation: ts)

The **tstart** command initiates a transaction. Depending on parameters, it may specify that the transaction can be restarted. Details are implementation dependent. Not available in all implementations.

6.23 use (abbreviation: **u**)

The **use** command tells the program which device or unit to use for input/output operations (**read**s and **write**s). The unit or device thus designated as the current input/output device remains in effect until changed by another **use** or an error occurs.

The **use** command may permit several implementation device options to be specified. Consult your user's guide for full details.

Figure 85 gives some GPL Mumps examples.

```
1    #!/usr/bin/mumps
2
3      open 1:"indata.dat,old"
4      if '$test write "Error on indata.dat."!, halt
5      open 2:"outdata.dat,new"
6      if '$test write "Error on outdata.dat.",! halt
7
8      set f=1
9      for  do   quit:f
10     . use 1
11     . read rec
12     . if '$test set f=1 quit
13     . use 2
14     . write rec,!
15
16     use 5
17
18     write "finished.",!
```

Figure 85 **Use** Examples

6.24 view (abbreviation: **v**)

Implementation defined. Often used as a debugging aid. Consult your vendor's guide for details. Not implemented in GPL Mumps.

6.25 write (abbreviation: w)

The **write** command transmits data to an output device or file. Output goes to the file or device associated with the current unit number (see *$io*). By the **use** command, however, data may be directed to another unit number or device and its associated file.

The **write** command takes as arguments either literal strings in quotes, numeric constants, variable names, both local and global, expressions and control codes for tab, new line and new page format operations.

The format control operations are the same as those discussed above for the **read** operation. Output is stream oriented: that is, each **write** does not begin on a new line: it begins where the last line left off. Wrap-around occurs at your terminal depending upon the current terminal monitor level width setting.

You may specify single character output by an asterisk followed by a decimal number. The system will send the ASCII character associated with the number you specify (e.g., *7 will send the *BELL* character). Figure 86 gives some examples.

```
1  #!/usr/bin/mumps
2      write "Name of Patient",?25,name
3      write !,"Age",?20,age
4      write *65,*66,*67,!   ; writes ABC
5      set i="10*2" write @i   ; writes 20
```

Figure 86 **Write** Examples

6.26 xecute (abbreviation: x)

The **xecute** command permits execution of strings as though they were lines of code. Figure 87 gives an example. Here, numbers 1 through 20 will be written to the current output device.

Strings can be constructed in your program, read in, or fetched from the global array database. When the actions specified by the string being executed have completed, control returns to the line containing the **xecute** command. If a **quit** command is executed, return to the line containing the **xecute** is immediate.

```
1  #!/usr/bin/mumps
2      set test="for i=1:1:20 write i,!"
3      xecute test
```

Figure 87 **Xecute** Example

7 Builtin/Intrinsic Variables

Mumps provides several builtin variables which are used to reflect the status of the system. Some of these may be set by the user, others are read-only.

7.1 $device (abbreviation: $d)

The status of the current device. This variable can be modified. Not available in all implementations. See vendor guide for details.

7.2 $ecode (abbreviation: $ec)

A list of the error codes for your system. This variable may be modified. Not available in all implementations. See vendor's guide for details.

7.3 $estack (abbreviation: $es)

Current number of stack levels for the current process. This values can be reset by the **new** command. Not available in all implementations. See vendor guide for details.

7.4 $etrap (abbreviation: $et)

The code to be executed the event of an error, usually a routine to be done or branched to. This value may be altered and stacked by means of the **new** command. Not available in all implementations. See vendor's guide for details.

7.5 $horolog (abbreviation: **$h**)

The *$h* built-in variable returns a string consisting of two numbers. The first is the number of days since December 31, 1840 (the founding date for the Massachusetts General Hospital) and the second is the number of seconds since the most recent midnight. The variable may not appear as the target of an assignment or read command.

7.6 $io (abbreviation: **$i**)

$io gives the current unit number. Mumps I/O is, at any given time, directed to a unit number. This is the unit from which all **read**s and **write**s will take place. If the user **open**s another unit number or device for other file operations, the **use** command is used to redirect **read** and **write** commands to this unit or device. The builtin *$io* variable reports the current i/o unit number. It may not appear as the target of an assignment statement or as an argument of a **read** command.

7.7 $job (abbreviation: **$j**)

The **$job** variable returns the system job number. In GPL Mumps, this is the Linux process PID in hexadecimal.

7.8 $key (abbreviation: $k)

The I/O control codes which ended the last read operation. See vendor's guide for details. Not available in all implementations.

7.9 $principal (abbreviation: $p)

The principal I/O device. Details are implementation dependent. Not available in all implementations.

7.10 $quit (abbreviation: $q)

Indicates (if *true* or 1) that the current block of code was called as an external function call, *false* otherwise. Consult your vendor's guide for details. Details are implementation dependent. Not available in all implementations.

7.11 $stack (abbreviation: $st)

The depth of the current process stack. Consult vendor's guide for details. Details are implementation dependent. Not available in all implementations.

7.12 $storage (abbreviation: $s)

Returns the amount of memory remaining in the interpreter available to run user programs. Implementation dependent.

7.13 $system (abbreviation: $sy)

Returns the current system identification. Details are implementation dependent. Not available in all implementations.

7.14 $test (abbreviation: $t)

The **$test** variable reflects the status after certain commands. Generally speaking, it is set to one (1) when the command succeeds and to zero (0) when the command fails. The value in $test remains until it is changed. Examples of commands that set *$test* are: **read**, **open**, and **if**.

7.15 $tlevel (abbreviation: $tl)

Returns the number of nested transactions. Details are implementation dependent. Not available in all implementations.

7.16 $trestart (abbreviation: $tr)

Number of times the current transaction has been restarted. Details are implementation dependent. Not available in all implementations.

7.17 $x

The *$x* variable gives an approximation of the current horizontal position of the record in the current unit number or device. For terminals, this is the horizontal cursor position. For other files, it is the number of characters since the start of the current record. The value of $x may be set by the **set** command but doing so does not result in a change to the hardware cursor.

7.18 $y

The $y variable gives the vertical cursor position of the current unit number or device. It is re-set to zero for each top of forms format control used.

7.19 $z...

Vendor specific implementation defined additional functions.

8 Structured System Variables

Structured system variables are used to communicate the current state of the system. Consult your vendor's guide for details. The approved list, as of the last (1995) standard is:

8.1 ^$character (abbreviation: ^$c)

Information on available and current character sets. Details are implementation dependent. Not available in all implementations.

8.2 ^$device (abbreviation: ^$d)

Information about current devices. Details are implementation dependent. Not available in all implementations.

8.3 ^$global (abbreviation: ^$g)

Information about global variables. Details are implementation dependent. Not available in all implementations.`

8.4 ^$job (abbreviation: ^$j)

Information about the current process. Details are implementation dependent. Not available in all implementations.

8.5 ^$lock (abbreviation: ^$l)

Information about current locks. Details are implementation dependent. Not available in all implementations.

8.6 ^$routine (abbreviation: ^$r)

Information about current routines. Details are implementation dependent. Not available in all implementations.

8.7 ^$system (abbreviation: ^$s)

Information about the current system. Details are implementation dependent. Not available in all implementations.

8.8 ^$z[...]

Vendor defined.

9 Builtin Functions

9.1 $ascii(e1) or $ascii(e1,i2)

$ascii returns the numeric value of an ASCII character. The string is specified in *e1*. If no *i2* is specified, the first character of *e1* is used. If *i2* is specified, the *i2*'th character of *e1* is chosen. Figure 88 gives several examples.

```
1   $ascii("ABC") YIELDS 65
2   $ascii("ABC",1) YIELDS 65
3   $ascii("ABC,2) YIELDS 66
4   $ascii("") YIELDS -1
```

Figure 88 *$Ascii()* Examples

9.2 $char(i1) or $char(i1,i2) or $char(i1,i2,...)

$char translates numeric arguments to ASCII character strings. Figure 89 gives examples.

```
1   $char(65) yields "A"
2   $char(65,66) yields "AB"
```

Figure 89 *$Char()* Examples

9.3 $data(vn)

$data() returns an integer which indicates whether the variable *vn* is defined. The value returned is 0 if *vn* is undefined, 1 if *vn* has data and has no associated array descendants; 10 if *vn* has no data does have descendants; and 11 is *vn* has data and has descendants. The argument *vn* may be either a local or global variable. Figure 90 gives examples.

```
1   set A(1,11)="foo"
2   set A(1,11,21)="bar"
3   $data(A(1))           ; yields 10
4   $data(A(1,11))        ; yields 11
5   $data(A(1,11,21))     ; yields    1
6   $data(A(1,11,22)      ; yields    0
```

Figure 90 *$Data()* Examples

9.4 $extract(e1,i2) or $extract(e1,i2,i3)

$extract returns a substring of the first argument. The substring begins at the position noted by the second operand. Note that character positions in Mumps strings are numbered from one, not zero as is common in other languages.

If the third operand is omitted, the substring consists only of the *i2*'th character of *e1*. If the third argument is present, the substring begins at position *i2* and ends at position *i3*.

If only *e1* is given, the function returns the first character of the string *e1*.

If *i3* specifies a position beyond the end of *e1*, the substring ends at the end of *e1*. Figure 91 gives examples.

The **$extract** function may be used on the right hand side of an assignment operator or in a **read** command. In these cases, the portion of the string determined by the parameters is replaced with the value from the left hand side of the assignment operator. The variable is padded, as needed, with blanks to accommodate the length implied by the second and third operands.

9.5 $find(e1,e2) or $find(e1,e2,i3)

$find() searches the first argument for an occurrence of the second argument. If one is found, the value returned is one greater than the end position of the second argument in the first argument. If *i3* is specified, the search begins at position *i3* in argument 1. If the second argument is not found, the value returned is 0. Mumps strings begin with position one, not zero. Figure 92 gives examples.

1	`$extract("ABC",2)`	`"B"`
2	`$extract("ABCDEF",3,5)`	`"CDE"`
3	`$extract("ABCDEF")`	`"A"`
4	`$extract("ABCDEF",5,10)`	`"EF"`
5	`set X="123456789" set $extract(X)="A"`	`"A23456789"`
6	`set X="123456789"`	
7	`set $extract(X,3,5)="xxxxx"`	`"12xxxxx6789"`
8	`set X="123" set $extract(X,5)="aaa"`	`"123 aaa"`
9	`kill X set $extract(X,3,5)="aaa"`	`"  aaa"`

Figure 91 *$Extract()* Examples

9.6 $fnumber(numexp,code[,int])

Returns a formatted representation of the first argument based on subsequent parameters. The parameter *code* is a character string consisting of zero or more of the codes shown in Figure 93.

The third argument, if present, is the number of places to the right of the decimal point.

1	`$find("ABC","B")`	yields 3
2	`$find("ABCABC","A",3)`	yields 5

Figure 92 *$Find()* Examples

9.7 $get(i1) or $get(i1,i2)

Returns the value of the local or global variable specified as the first operand if it exists or a default value, specified as the second operand, if it does not. If the second operand is omitted, an empty string is used as the default value.

9.8 $justify(e1,i2) or $justify(e1,i2,i3)

$justify() right justifies the first argument in a string field whose length is given by the second argument. In the two operand form, the first argument is interpreted as a string. In the three argument form, the first argument is right justified in a field whose length is given by the second argument with *i3* decimal places. The three argument form imposes a numeric interpretation upon the first argument. Figure 94 gives examples.

P (or p)	Surround the value of numexp with parentheses if negative, spaces if positive.
T (or t)	Trailing minus sign if negative or blank if positive.
, (comma character)	Insert commas into resulting number after every three significant digits.
+ (plus sign)	Force plus sign on positive values
- (minus sign)	Suppress minus sign on negative values.

Figure 93 *$Fnumber()* Format Codes

1	$justify(39,3)	YIELDS " 39"
2	$justify("TEST",7)	YIELDS " TEST"
3	$justify(39,4,1)	YIELDS "39.0"

Figure 94 *$Justify()* Examples

9.9 $len(e1) or $len(e1,e2)

The *$len()* function returns the string length of its argument. Figure 95 gives examples.

1	$len("ABC")	YIELDS 3
2	$len(22.5)	YIELDS 4
3	$len("abcxxabcxxabc","abc")	YIELDS 3

Figure 95 *$Len()* Examples

If a second argument is given, the function returns the number of non-overlapping occurrences of *e2* in *e1* plus 1.

9.10 $name(vn[,count])

The *$name()* function returns the evaluated name of a variable with all or some of its subscripts. Figure 96 gives examples.

```
 1   #!/usr/bin/mumps
 2       set a=1,b=2,c=3,d=4
 3       set x(1,2,3,4)=99
 4       write $name(x(a,b,c,d)),!
 5       write $name(x(a,b,c,d),99),!
 6       write $name(x(a,b,c,d),4),!
 7       write $name(x(a,b,c,d),3),!
 8       write $name(x(a,b,c,d),2),!
 9       write $name(x(a,b,c,d),1),!
10       write $name(x(a,b,c,d),0),!
11
12       set ^x(1,2,3,4)=99
13       write $name(^x(a,b,c,d)),!
14       write $name(^x(a,b,c,d),99),!
15       write $name(^x(a,b,c,d),4),!
16       write $name(^x(a,b,c,d),3),!
17       write $name(^x(a,b,c,d),2),!
18       write $name(^x(a,b,c,d),1),!
19       write $name(^x(a,b,c,d),0),!

output:

x(1,2,3,4)
x(1,2,3,4)
x(1,2,3,4)
x(1,2,3)
x(1,2)
x(1)
x

^x(1,2,3,4)
^x(1,2,3,4)
^x(1,2,3,4)
^x(1,2,3)
^x(1,2)
^x(1)
^x
```

Figure 96 *$Name()* Examples

9.11 $next(vn) (deprecated)

Similar to **$order()**. This was the original function used to
navigate from one sibling array node to the next. To find the
initial node, *$next(-1)* was used. Nodes would be returned in
strict ASCII collating sequence. The last node was indicated by
the return of the value -1. Negative subscripts were not normally
permitted. This function is deprecated.

9.12 $order(vn[,d])

The *$order()* function replaced *$next().* It traverses an array
from one sibling node to the next in key ascending or descending
order. The result returned is the next value of the last index of the
global or local array given as the first argument. The default
traversal is in key ascending order except if the optional second
argument is present and evaluates to "-1" in which case the
traversal is in descending key order. If the second argument is

present and has a value of "1", the traversal will be in ascending key order (the default). Numeric subscripts should be retrieved in numeric order. Consult your user's guide. Figure 97 gives several examples.

9.13 $piece(e1,e2,i3) or $piece(e1,e2,i3,i4)

The *$piece()* function returns a substring of the first argument delimited by the instances of the second argument.

The substring returned in the three argument case is that substring of the first argument that lies between the $i3^{th}$ minus one and $i3^{th}$ occurrence of the second argument.

In the four argument form, the string returned is that substring of the first argument delimited by the $i3^{th}$ minus one instance of the second argument and the $i4^{th}$ instance of the second argument.

If only two arguments are given, $i3$ is assumed to be 1. For example, see Figure 98.

```
1    #!/use/bin/mumps
2        for i=1:1:9 s ^a(i)=i
3        set ^b(1)=1
4        set ^b(2)=-1
5        write "expect (next higher) 1 ",$order(^a("")),!
6        write "expect (next lower) 9 ",$order(^a(""),-1),!
7        write "expect 1 ",$order(^a(""),^b(1)),!
8        write "expect 9 ",$order(^a(""),^b(2)),!
9        set i=0,j=1
10       write "expect 1 ",$order(^a(""),j),!
11       write "expect 9 ",$order(^a(""),-j),!
12       write "expect 1 ",$order(^a(""),i+j),!
13       write "expect 9 ",$order(^a(""),i-j),!
14
15       set i=""
16       write "expect 1 2 3 ... 9",!
17       for  do  quit:i=""
18       . set i=$order(^a(i),1)
19       . if i="" quit
20       . write i,!
21
22       set i=""
23       write "expect 9 8 7 ... 1",!
24       for  do  quit:i=""
25       . set i=$order(^a(i),-1)
26       . if i="" quit
27       . write i,!
```

Figure 97 *$Order()* Examples

$piece() can be used on the left hand side of a **set** command or as an argument in a **read** command. In these cases, the first argument must be a local or global variable. The contents of this variable are altered to the value of the right hand side of the **set** statement or the value read by the **read** statement. The entire

contents of the local or global variable are not altered, only the part which would have been extracted by the $piece() function.

9.14 $qlength(e1)

Returns the number of subscripts in the variable name. For example, see Figure 99 which writes 3, 2, and 0.

9.15 $qsubscript(e1,e2)

The $qsubscript() function returns a portion of the array reference given by e1. If the second argument is -1, the environment is returned (if defined), if 0, the name of the global array is returned. For values greater than 0, the value of the associated subscript is returned. If a value exceeds the number of indices, an empty string is returned. See Figure 99 for examples. Here, the program prints the current directory (environments are defined as the current directory in the GPL Mumps implementation), ^a, 1, 2, and 3 respectively. Note: the variables or values of the subscripts must be valid.

```
1    $piece("A.BX.Y",".",2) => "BX"
2    $piece("A.BX.Y",".",1) => "A"
3    $piece("A.BX.Y",".",2,3) => "BX.Y"
```

Figure 98 $Piece() Examples

9.16 $query(e1)

The $query() function returns the next array element in the array space. The first and only argument to $query() is a string representation of a global or local array. The value returned is the next ascending entry in the array space. An empty string is returned when there are no more array references to return. Figure 101 gives examples.

```
1    #!/usr/bin/mumps
2        set i=1,j=2,k=3
3        set b(1)=99
4        write $qlength("^a(i,j,k)"),!
5        write $qlength("a(b(1),2)"),!
6        write $qlength("^a"),!
```

Figure 99 $Qlength() Examples

```
1    #!/usr/bin/mumps
2        set i=1,j=2,k=3,m="k"
3        write $qsubscript("^a(i,j,k)",-1),!
4        write $qsubscript("^a(i,j,k)",0),!
5        write $qsubscript("^a(i,j,k)",1),!
6        write $qsubscript("^a(i,j,k)",2),!
7        write $qsubscript("^a(i,j,@m)",3),!
```

Figure 100 $Qsubscript() Examples

```
1    #!/usr/bin/mumps
2
3      ; assumes global array database is completely empty.
4
5      ; create a test data base
6
7        kill ^a
8        for i=1:1:3 do
9        . for j=1:1:3  do
10       .. for k=1:1:3 do
11       ... set ^a(i,j,k)=i
12
13       set x="^a"
14
15       set f=0
16       for  do quit:f
17       . set x=$query(@x)
18       . if x="" set f=1 quit
19       . write "example 1 ",x,!
20
21       set j=3
22       write "example 2 ",$query(@"^a(j)"),!
23       write "example 3 ",$query(@"^a(2*j-j)"),!
24       set a="2+1"
25       write "example 4 ",$query(@"^a(@a)"),!
26       set z="^a(1)"
27       set ^a(1)="^a(2)"
28       write "example 5 ",$query(@z),!
29       set f=0
30       set a="^a(1)"
31       for  do  quit:f
32       . set a=$query(@a)
33       . if a="" set f=1 quit
34       . write "example 6 ",a," -> "
35       . write $qsubscript(@a,0)," "
36       . write $qsubscript(@a,1)," "
37       . write $qsubscripta(@a,2)," "
38       . write $qsubscript(@a,3),!

output:

example 1 ^a("1","1","1")
example 1 ^a("1","1","2")
example 1 ^a("1","1","3")
example 1 ^a("1","2","1")
...
example 4 ^a("3","1","1")
example 5 ^a("1","1","1")
example 6 ^a(1) -> ^a 1
example 6 ^a("1","1","1") -> ^a 1 1 1
example 6 ^a("1","1","2") -> ^a 1 1 2
example 6 ^a("1","1","3") -> ^a 1 1 3
...
example 6 ^a("3","3","2") -> ^a 3 3 2
example 6 ^a("3","3","3") -> ^a 3 3 3
```

Figure 101 $Query() Examples

9.17 $random(i1)

$random() returns an integer in the range zero through *i1*-1. For example, *$random(100)* yields a value between 0 and 99. The random number generator is seeded with the time of day each time the interpreter is invoked. See also: *$zsrand()*.

9.18 $reverse(i1)

The *$reverse()* function reverses the order of the characters in the argument string. Figure 102 gives an example.

9.19 $select(t1:e1,t2:e2,...tn:en)

The *$select()* function takes a variable number of arguments delimited by commas. Each argument consists of three parts: a logical expression followed by a colon, followed by a result expression. The function evaluates each logical expression in the order in which they appear (shown above as *t1, t2, ...tn*). If a logical expression is *true*, the result of the expression (*e1, e2, ... en*) is evaluated and becomes the value for the function. It is an error if all logical expressions evaluate to *false*. Evaluation ends at the first *true* expression. Figure 103 gives an example.

9.20 $translate(S1,S2) or $translate(S1,S2,S3)

If only two strings are given, characters appearing in the second string are removed from the first string. If three strings appear and the second and third string are of the same length, characters from the first string that appear in the second string are replaced by their counterparts from the third string. If the second string is longer than the third string, the characters from the second string which have no counterpart in the third string are removed. A "counterpart" is a character equally offset in the third string to the character in the second string. Figure 104 gives examples.

```
1    #!/usr/bin/mumps
2      set x="now is the time"
3      write $reverse(x),!

the above writes: emit eht si won
```

Figure 102 $Reverse() Examples

```
1    #!/usr/bin/mumps
2
3      set i=10,j=20,k=30,x=20
4      write $select(x=i:"aaa",x=20:"bbb",x=20:"ccc"),!

the above writes bbb
```

Figure 103 $Select() Example

```
1    #!/usr/bin/mumps
2      write $translate("ABCDEFG","EF"),!
3      write $translate("ABCDEFG","EF","ef"),!

output:

ABCDG
ABCDefG
```

Figure 104 *$Translate()* Examples

10 Programming Examples

10.1 The Medical Subject Headings (MeSH) Example

MeSH (Medical Subject Headings) is a controlled vocabulary hierarchical indexing and classification system developed by the National Library of Medicine (NLM). The MeSH codes are used to code medical records and literature as part of an ongoing research project at the NLM.

The following examples make use of the 2003 MeSH Tree Hierarchy. Newer versions, essentially similar to these, are available from NLM.

Note: *for clinical purposes, this copy of the MeSH hierarchy is out of date and should not be used for clinical decision making. It is used here purely as an example to illustrate a hierarchical index.* (warning required by NLM)

The 2003 MeSH file contains approximately 40,000 entries. Each line consists of text along with codes which place the text into a hierarchical context. Figure 105 contains a sample from the 2003 MeSH file.

```
Body Regions;A01
Abdomen;A01.047
Abdominal Cavity;A01.047.025
Peritoneum;A01.047.025.600
Douglas' Pouch;A01.047.025.600.225
Mesentery;A01.047.025.600.451
Mesocolon;A01.047.025.600.451.535
Omentum;A01.047.025.600.573
Peritoneal Cavity;A01.047.025.600.678
Retroperitoneal Space;A01.047.025.750
Abdominal Wall;A01.047.050
Groin;A01.047.365
Inguinal Canal;A01.047.412
Umbilicus;A01.047.849
Back;A01.176
Lumbosacral Region;A01.176.519
Sacrococcygeal Region;A01.176.780
Breast;A01.236
Nipples;A01.236.500
Extremities;A01.378
Amputation Stumps;A01.378.100
```

Figure 105 Sample MeSH Hierarchy

The format of the MeSH table is:

1. a short text description
2. a semi-colon, and
3. a sequence of decimal point separated codes.

The MeSH codes are an example of a *controlled vocabulary*. That is, a collection of indexing terms that are preselected, defined and authorized by an authoritative source.

10.2 Building a MeSH Structured Global Array

First, our goal here is to write a program to build a global array tree whose structure corresponds to the MeSH hierarchy. In this tree, each successive index in the global array reference will be a successive code from an entry in the 2003 MeSH hierarchy. The text part of each MeSH entry will be stored as the global array data value at both terminal and intermediate indexing levels.

To do this, we want to run a program consisting of Mumps assignment statements similar to the fragment shown in Figure 106. In this example, the code identifiers from the MeSH hierarchy become global array indices and the corresponding text becomes assigned values.

```
1    set ^mesh("A01")="Body Regions"
2    set ^mesh("A01","047")="Abdomen"
3    set ^mesh("A01","047","025")="Abdomenal Cavity"
4    set ^mesh("A01","047","025","600")="Peritoneum"
5    set ^mesh("A01","047","365")="Groin"
     .
     .
     .
```

Figure 106 Global Array Commands

A graphical representation of this can be seen in Figure 10. which depicts the MeSH tree and the corresponding Mumps assignment statements needed to create the structured global array corresponding to the diagram.

A program to build a MeSH tree is shown in Figure 107. However, rather than being a program consisting of several thousand Mumps assignment statements, instead we use the Mumps indirection facility to write a short Mumps program that reads the MeSH file and dynamically generates and executes several thousand assignment statements.

The program in Figure 107, in a loop (lines 8 through 39), reads a line from the file *mesh2003.txt* (line 10). On lines 12 and 13 the part of the MeSH entry prior and following the semi-colon are extracted into the strings *key* and *code*, respectively. The loop on lines 17 through 19 extracts each decimal point separated element of the code into successively numbered elements of the local array *x*. On line 23 a string is assigned to the variable *z* which will be the initial portion of the global array reference to be constructed.

On line 30 elements of the array *x* are concatenated onto *z* with encompassing quotes and separating commas. On line 31 the final element of array *x* is added along with a closing parenthesis, an assignment operator and the value of *key* and the text is prepended with a Mumps *set* command. Now the contents of *z* look like a Mumps assignment statement which is executed on line 39 thus creating the entry in the database. The *xecute* command in Mumps causes the string passed to it to be treated and executed as Mumps code.

```
1    #!/usr/bin/mumps
2    ; BuildMeshTree.mps
3
4        kill ^mesh
5        open 1:"mtrees2003.txt,old"
6        if '$test write "mtrees2003.txt not found",! halt
7        set f=0
8        for  do   quit:f
9        . use 1
10       . read a
11       . if '$test set f=1 quit
12       . set key=$piece(a,";",1)  ; text description
13       . set code=$piece(a,";",2) ; everything else
14       . if key=""!(code="") set f=1 quit
15
16       . set f1=0
17       . for i=1:1 do   quit:f1
18       .. set x(i)=$piece(code,".",i) ; extract code numbers
19       .. if x(i)="" set f1=1 quit
20
21       . set i=i-1
22       . use 5
23       . set z="^mesh("   ; begin building a global reference
24
25   ;
26   ; build a reference like ^mesh("A01","047","025","600)
27   ; by concatenating quotes, codes, quotes, and commas onto z
28   ;
29
30       . for j=1:1:i-1 set z=z_""""_x(j)_""","
31       . set z="set "_z_""""_x(i)_""")="""_key_""""
32
33   ;
34   ; z now looks like set ^mesh("A01","047")="Abdomen"
35   ; now execute the text
36   ;
37
38       . write z,!
39       . xecute z
40
41       close 1
42       use 5
43       write "done",!
44       halt
```

Figure 107 MeSH Global Array

Note that to embed a double-quote character (") into a string, you place two immediately adjacent double-quote characters into the string. Thus: """" means a string of length one containing a double-quote character.

Line 11 uses the OR operator (!) to test if either *key* or *code* is the empty string. Note that parentheses are needed in this predicate since expressions in Mumps are executed left-to-right without precedence. Without parentheses, the predicate would evaluate as if it had been written as :

```
((key="")!code)=""
```

which would yield a completely different result!

Line 30 uses the concatenation operator (_) on the local array $x(j)$. Local arrays should be used as little as possible as access to them is through the Mumps run-time symbol table which can be slow especially if there are a large number of variables or array elements in the current program.

The *close* command on line 41 releases the file associated with unit 1 and makes unit 1 available for re-use. Closing a file opened for input is not strictly needed unless you want to reuse the unit number. Closing a file open for output, however, is desirable in order to flush the internal system buffers to disk. If the program crashes before an output file is closed, it is possible to lose data.

```
1    set ^mesh("A01")="Body Regions"
2    set ^mesh("A01","047")="Abdomen"
3    set ^mesh("A01","047","025")="Abdominal Cavity"
4    set ^mesh("A01","047","025","600")="Peritoneum"
5    set ^mesh("A01","047","025","600","225")="Douglas' Pouch"
6    set ^mesh("A01","047","025","600","451")="Mesentery"
7    set ^mesh("A01","047","025","600","451","535")="Mesocolon"
8    set ^mesh("A01","047","025","600","573")="Omentum"
9    set ^mesh("A01","047","025","600","678")="Peritoneal Cavity"
10   set ^mesh("A01","047","025","750")="Retroperitoneal Space"
11   set ^mesh("A01","047","050")="Abdominal Wall"
12   set ^mesh("A01","047","365")="Groin"
13   set ^mesh("A01","047","412")="Inguinal Canal"
14   set ^mesh("A01","047","849")="Umbilicus"
15   set ^mesh("A01","176")="Back"
16   set ^mesh("A01","176","519")="Lumbosacral Region"
17   set ^mesh("A01","176","780")="Sacrococcygeal Region"
18   set ^mesh("A01","236")="Breast"
19   set ^mesh("A01","236","500")="Nipples"
20   set ^mesh("A01","378")="Extremities"
21   set ^mesh("A01","378","100")="Amputation Stumps"
22   set ^mesh("A01","378","610")="Lower Extremity"
23   set ^mesh("A01","378","610","100")="Buttocks"
24   set ^mesh("A01","378","610","250")="Foot"
25   set ^mesh("A01","378","610","250","149")="Ankle"
26   set ^mesh("A01","378","610","250","300")="Forefoot, Human"
27   set ^mesh("A01","378","610","250","300","480")="Metatarsus"
     .
     .
     .
```

Figure 108 Creating the Mesh tree

The output of the program in Figure 107 is shown in Figure 108. Line 38 writes the text of the created mumps *set* command. These are the commands executed by the *xecute* command on line 39.

10.3 Displaying the MeSH Global Array Part I

Now that the MeSH global array has been created, the question is, how to print it, properly indented to show the tree structure of the data.

The program in Figure 109 gives one way to print the global array and the results are shown in Figure 110. In this example we have successively nested loops to print data at lower levels. When data is printed, it is indented by 0, 5, 10, and 15 spaces to reflect the level of the data.

On Line 4 the process begins by finding successive values of the first index of *^mesh*. Each iteration of this outermost loop will yield, in alphabetic order, a new top level value until there are none remaining. These are placed in the local variable *lev1*.

The program then advances to line 6 which will yield successive values of all second level codes subordinate to the current top level code (*lev1*). Each of these is placed in *lev2*. The second level codes are printed on line 7 indented by 5 spaces.

```
1    #!/usr/bin/mumps
2    ; BasicMtreePrint.mps
3
4        for lev1=$order(^mesh(lev1)) do
5        . write lev1," ",^mesh(lev1),!
6        . for lev2=$order(^mesh(lev1,lev2)) do
7        .. write ?5,lev2," ",^mesh(lev1,lev2),!
8        .. for lev3=$order(^mesh(lev1,lev2,lev3)) do
9        ... write ?10,lev3," ",^mesh(lev1,lev2,lev3),!
10       ... for lev4=$order(^mesh(lev1,lev2,lev3,lev4)) do
11       .... write ?15,lev4," ",^mesh(lev1,lev2,lev3,lev4),!
```

Figure 109 Print the MeSH tree

```
A01 Body Regions
     047 Abdomen
             025 Abdominal Cavity
                     600 Peritoneum
                     750 Retroperitoneal Space
             050 Abdominal Wall
             365 Groin
             412 Inguinal Canal
             849 Umbilicus
     176 Back
             519 Lumbosacral Region
             780 Sacrococcygeal Region
     236 Breast
             500 Nipples
     378 Extremities
```

```
              100 Amputation Stumps
              610 Lower Extremity
                      100 Buttocks
                      250 Foot
                      400 Hip
                      450 Knee
                      500 Leg
                      750 Thigh
              800 Upper Extremity
                      075 Arm
                      090 Axilla
                      420 Elbow
                      585 Forearm
                      667 Hand
                      750 Shoulder
      456 Head
          313 Ear
          505 Face
                  173 Cheek
                  259 Chin
                  420 Eye
                  580 Forehead
                  631 Mouth
                  733 Nose
                  750 Parotid Region
          810 Scalp
          830 Skull Base
                  150 Cranial Fossa, Anterior
                  165 Cranial Fossa, Middle
                  200 Cranial Fossa, Posterior
      598 Neck
      673 Pelvis
          600 Pelvic Floor
      719 Perineum
      911 Thorax
          800 Thoracic Cavity
                  500 Mediastinum
                  650 Pleural Cavity
          850 Thoracic Wall
      960 Viscera
A02 Musculoskeletal System
      165 Cartilage
          165 Cartilage, Articular
          207 Ear Cartilages
          410 Intervertebral Disk
          507 Laryngeal Cartilages
                  083 Arytenoid Cartilage
                  211 Cricoid Cartilage
                  411 Epiglottis
                  870 Thyroid Cartilage
          590 Menisci, Tibial
          639 Nasal Septum
      340 Fascia
          424 Fascia Lata
      513 Ligaments
          170 Broad Ligament
          514 Ligaments, Articular
                  100 Anterior Cruciate Ligament
                  162 Collateral Ligaments
                  287 Ligamentum Flavum
```

```
350 Longitudinal Ligaments
475 Patellar Ligament
600 Posterior Cruciate Ligament
          . . .
```

Figure 110 Printed Mesh tree

The process continues for levels 3 and 4. If there are no codes at a given level, the loop at that level terminates and flow is returned to the outer loop. The inner loops, if any, are not executed.

10.4 Printing the MeSH Global Array Part II

In the example in Figure 111, we first set a local variable x to ^mesh, the unindexed name of the MeSH global array. In the loop on lines 6 through 10, the variable x is passed as an argument to the builtin function $query() which returns the next ascendant global array key in the database. These can be seen in the right hand column output in Figure 112. These are re-assigned to the variable x.

The program in Figure 111 presents a more general function to print the ^mesh hierarchy as shown in the output in Figure 112.

```
1    #!/usr/bin/mumps
2    ; AdvancedMtreePrint.mps
3
4      set x="^mesh"
5      set f=0
6      for  do   quit:f
7      . set x=$query(@x)
8      . if x="" set f=1 quit
9      . set i=$qlength(@x)
10     . write ?i*2," ",$qsubscript(x,i)," ",@x,?50,x,!
```

Figure 111 Alternate MeSH Tree Print

In line 9 the number of subscripts in the global array reference in variable x is assigned to the local variable i. In line 10 this number is used to indent the output by twice the number os spaces as there are subscripts (?i*2).

The $qsubscript() function returns the value of the ith subscript (e.g., A01). The expression @x evaluates the string in variable x which, since it is a global array reference, evaluates to the value stored at the global array node which is the MeSH text description. The actual MeSH global array reference is then printed in a column to the right.

10.5 Displaying Global Arrays in Key Order

The Mumps function $query() can be used access the b-tree keys in the order in which they are actually stored in sequential key order as shown in Figure 113.

The example program shown in program in Figure 114 passes to *$query()* a string containing a global array reference. The function returns the next ascending global array reference in the file system. Eventually, it will run out of *^mesh* references and receive an empty string. Consequently, it tests to determine if it received the empty string.

```
A01 Body Regions                       ^mesh("A01","047")
  047 Abdomen                          ^mesh("A01","047","025")
    025 Abdominal Cavity               ^mesh("A01","047","025","600")
      600 Peritoneum                   ^mesh("A01","047","025","600","225")
        225 Douglas' Pouch             ^mesh("A01","047","025","600","451")
        451 Mesentery                  ^mesh("A01","047","025","600","451","535")
        535 Mesocolon                  ^mesh("A01","047","025","600","573")
        573 Omentum                    ^mesh("A01","047","025","600","678")
        678 Peritoneal Cavity          ^mesh("A01","047","025","750")
      750 Retroperitoneal Space        ^mesh("A01","047","050")
    050 Abdominal Wall                 ^mesh("A01","047","365")
    365 Groin                          ^mesh("A01","047","412")
    412 Inguinal Canal                 ^mesh("A01","047","849")
    849 Umbilicus                      ^mesh("A01","176")
  176 Back                             ^mesh("A01","176","519")
    519 Lumbosacral Region             ^mesh("A01","176","780")
    780 Sacrococcygeal Region          ^mesh("A01","236")
  236 Breast                           ^mesh("A01","236","500")
    500 Nipples                        ^mesh("A01","378")
  378 Extremities                      ^mesh("A01","378","100")
    100 Amputation Stumps              ^mesh("A01","378","610")
    610 Lower Extremity                ^mesh("A01","378","610","100")
      100 Buttocks                     ^mesh("A01","378","610","250")
      250 Foot                         ^mesh("A01","378","610","250","149")
        149 Ankle                      ^mesh("A01","378","610","250","300")
        300 Forefoot, Human            ^mesh("A01","378","610","250","300","480")
          480 Metatarsus               ^mesh("A01","378","610","250","300","792")
          792 Toes                     ^mesh("A01","378","610","250","300","792","380")
            380 Hallux                 ^mesh("A01","378","610","250","510")
        510 Heel                       ^mesh("A01","378","610","400")
      400 Hip                          ^mesh("A01","378","610","450")
      450 Knee                         ^mesh("A01","378","610","500")
      500 Leg                          ^mesh("A01","378","610","750")
      750 Thigh                        ^mesh("A01","378","800")
    800 Upper Extremit                 ^mesh("A01","378","800","075")
      075 Arm                          ^mesh("A01","378","800","090")
      090 Axilla                       ^mesh("A01","378","800","420")
      420 Elbow                        ^mesh("A01","378","800","585")
      585 Forearm                      ^mesh("A01","378","800","667")
      667 Hand                         ^mesh("A01","378","800","667","430")
        430 Fingers                    ^mesh("A01","378","800","667","430","705")
          705 Thumb                    ^mesh("A01","378","800","667","715")
        715 Wrist                      ^mesh("A01","378","800","750")
      750 Shoulder                     ^mesh("A01","456")
  456 Head                             ^mesh("A01","456","313")
    313 Ear                            ^mesh("A01","456","505")
    505 Face                           ^mesh("A01","456","505","173")
      173 Cheek                        ^mesh("A01","456","505","259")
      259 Chin                         ^mesh("A01","456","505","420")
      420 Eye                          ^mesh("A01","456","505","420","338")
        338 Eyebrows                   ^mesh("A01","456","505","420","504")
        504 Eyelids                    ^mesh("A01","456","505","420","504","421")
          421 Eyelashes                ^mesh("A01","456","505","580")
      580 Forehead                     ^mesh("A01","456","505","631")
      631 Mouth                        ^mesh("A01","456","505","631","515")
```

Figure 112 Alternative MeSH Print

```
^mesh("A01")
^mesh("A01","047")
^mesh("A01","047","025")
^mesh("A01","047","025","600")
^mesh("A01","047","025","600","225")
^mesh("A01","047","025","600","451")
^mesh("A01","047","025","600","451","535")
```

```
^mesh("A01","047","025","600","573")
^mesh("A01","047","025","600","678")
^mesh("A01","047","025","750")
^mesh("A01","047","050")
^mesh("A01","047","365")
^mesh("A01","047","412")
^mesh("A01","047","849")
^mesh("A01","176")
```

Figure 113 MeSH Global Array Codes

Note: the line:

```
. write x,?50,@x,!
```

displays the global array reference in variable x and then prints the contents of the node at x by evaluating the global array reference (@x). Evaluation of a variable yields the value of the variable.

```
1    #!/usr/bin/mumps
2    ; AdvancedMtreePrint2.mps
3
4       set x="^mesh"   ; build the first index
5       for  do
6       . set x=$query(@x) ; get next array reference
7       . if x="" break
8       . write x,?50,@x
```

Figure 114 Print MeSH Global

The output from Figure 114 appears in Figure 115.

10.6 KWIC Index

KWIC, Key Word In Context, indices have been used for many years to show an alphabetic listing of terms in their original context. Normally KWIC indices are used with journal titles and, on each line, is a reference to the page number where the original article appears. A user looking for articles about term x would find the term in the index and scan the titles in which it occurred looking for those titles which most fit the search. Each time a word appears in a title, it will appear in the listing with that title. If a title has ten unique words, the title will appear ten times in the KWIC index.

In this case, we display an alphabetical listing of the words from from John Dryden's translation of the Aeneid with words in their original context. Such an index might be used by linguists to study

^mesh("A01")	Body Regions
^mesh("A01","047")	Abdomen
^mesh("A01","047","025")	Abdominal Cavity
^mesh("A01","047","025","600")	Peritoneum
^mesh("A01","047","025","600","225")	Douglas' Pouch
^mesh("A01","047","025","600","451")	Mesentery
^mesh("A01","047","025","600","451","535")	Mesocolon
^mesh("A01","047","025","600","573")	Omentum

```
^mesh("A01","047","025","600","678")          Peritoneal Cavity
^mesh("A01","047","025","750")                Retroperitoneal Space
^mesh("A01","047","050")                      Abdominal Wall
^mesh("A01","047","365")                      Groin
^mesh("A01","047","412")                      Inguinal Canal
^mesh("A01","047","849")                      Umbilicus
^mesh("A01","176")                            Back
^mesh("A01","176","519")                      Lumbosacral Region
^mesh("A01","176","780")                      Sacrococcygeal Region
^mesh("A01","236")                            Breast
^mesh("A01","236","500")                      Nipples
^mesh("A01","378")                            Extremities
^mesh("A01","378","100")                      Amputation Stumps
^mesh("A01","378","610")                      Lower Extremity
^mesh("A01","378","610","100")                Buttocks
^mesh("A01","378","610","250")                Foot
^mesh("A01","378","610","250","149")          Ankle
^mesh("A01","378","610","250","300")          Forefoot, Human
^mesh("A01","378","610","250","300","480")    Metatarsus
^mesh("A01","378","610","250","300","792")    Toes
^mesh("A01","378","610","250","300","792","3  Hallux
80")                                          Heel
^mesh("A01","378","610","250","510")          Hip
^mesh("A01","378","610","400")                Knee
^mesh("A01","378","610","450")                Leg
^mesh("A01","378","610","500")                Thigh
^mesh("A01","378","610","750")                Upper Extremity
^mesh("A01","378","800")                      Arm
^mesh("A01","378","800","075")                Axilla
^mesh("A01","378","800","090")                Elbow
^mesh("A01","378","800","420")                Forearm
^mesh("A01","378","800","585")                Hand
^mesh("A01","378","800","667")                Fingers
^mesh("A01","378","800","667","430")          Thumb
^mesh("A01","378","800","667","430","705")    Wrist
^mesh("A01","378","800","667","715")          Shoulder
^mesh("A01","378","800","750")
```

Figure 115 MeSH Global Printed

the meaning of words in their original context as they existed in the seventeenth century.

Input to the program in Figure 116 is from *stdin* (GPL Mumps Mumps unit 5). The program processes each line and writes a modified line to a temporary file named *tmp1.txt* This file is sorted by the system *sort* routine using the non-standard GPL Mumps extended command **shell** which executes a Linux command while the Mumps program waits. Most versions of Mumps have a similar facility. If this is not available, the program in Figure 116 would need to be broken into two parts and run serially with the *sort* invoked between the two steps. For simplicity, the **shell** command version is shown here.

The *sort* reads *tmp1.txt* and write *tmp2.txt* which is subsequently read by the Mumps program. The final output of the program is written to a file named *kwic.txt*.

Initially (lines 2 & 3) the program opens *tmp1.txt* for output and checks that the **open** worked.

A flag f is set to zero on line 6. Lines 7 through 22 are constitute the loop to process each input line. The loop continues until the flag f becomes true (1) which halts the loop (line 7).

Lines 8 through 13 read a line, check for end of input, and place the individual words from the line into the array w. The number of words in the array plus one is in the variable i after the loop on lines 11 through 13. In this loop, i increments for each iteration. Line 12 extracts the *ith* piece of the input lime delimited by blanks. On line 13, special characters ((): , .";-) are removed from the word. Note the two instances of the double quote - they count as one instance.

Lines 14 through 22 compose and write to the temporary file. They process each word in the array w (lines 15 through 22). If a word is less than four characters in length, it is skipped and no output line will be generated. Otherwise, the word is written at the beginning of the output line followed by enough blanks to make 30 characters (it's assumed that no word will be longer than 29 characters. In Position 30 a pound sign is placed. The pound sign is a delimiter. It does not appear anywhere in the text.

Lines18 through 21 create two strings x and y where x is the part of the line following the key word $w(j)$ and y is the part of the line preceding $w(j)$. These strings are formed by concatenating words and blanks together.

Line 22 writes out the first part of the line, the word in $w(j)$ and the last part of the line. The tabs are set to accommodate the different starting points on the line due to differing lengths of the first part. The effect is to place the word in the same place on the line.

After the file *tmp1.txt* has been written, it is closed and sorted with the output going to *tmp2.txt*. The *sort* function will be based on the initial word on the line which is in the first 29 positions.

Next, the sorted *tmp2.txt* is opened for input and *kwic.txt* is opened for output (lines 28 through 31). Input lines are read and written (lines 34 and 35) except the leading part of the input, up to the pound sign, is not written.

Samples of the input and output are given.

```
1    #!/usr/bin/mumps
2
3      open 1:"tmp1.txt,new"
4      if '$test write "File open error,!" halt
5
6      set f=0
7      for  do   quit:f
8      . use 5
```

```
9    . read in
10   . if '$test set f=1 quit
11   . for i=1:1 do  if $len(w(i))=0 quit
12   .. set x=$piece(in," ",i)
13   .. set w(i)=$translate(x,"():,.""";-")
14   . use 1
15   . for j=1:1:i do
16   .. if $len(w(j))<4 quit
17   .. write w(j),?30,"#"
18   .. set x=""
19   .. for k=j+1:1:i set x=x_w(k)_" "
20   .. set y=""
21   .. for k=j-1:-1:1 set y=w(k)_" "_y
22   .. write ?(85-$len(y)),y,?85,w(j)," ",x,!
23
24   close 1
25
26   shell sort < tmp1.txt > tmp2.txt
27
28   open 1:"tmp2.txt,old"
29   if '$test write "temp file error",! halt
30   open 2:"kwic.txt,new"
31   if '$test write "temp file error",! halt
32
33    for  do
34   . use 1 read in if '$test close 1,2 halt
35   . use 2 write $piece(in,"#",2),!
```

Input:

```
Arms, and the man I sing, who, forc'd by fate,
And haughty Juno's unrelenting hate,
Expell'd and exil'd, left the Trojan shore.
Long labors, both by sea and land, he bore,
And in the doubtful war, before he won
The Latian realm, and built the destin'd town;
His banish'd gods restor'd to rites divine,
And settled sure succession in his line,
From whence the race of Alban fathers come,
And the long glories of majestic Rome.
O Muse! the causes and the crimes relate;
What goddess was provok'd, and whence her hate;
For what offense the Queen of Heav'n began
To persecute so brave, so just a man;
Involv'd his anxious life in endless cares,
Expos'd to wants, and hurried into wars!
Can heav'nly minds such high resentment show,
Or exercise their spite in human woe?
Against the Tiber's mouth, but far away,
An ancient town was seated on the sea;
A Tyrian colony; the people made
Stout for the war, and studious of their trade:
Carthage the name; belov'd by Juno more
Than her own Argos, or the Samian shore.
Here stood her chariot; here, if Heav'n were kind,
The seat of awful empire she design'd.
Yet she had heard an ancient rumor fly,
(Long cited by the people of the sky,)
...
```

```
Output:

                        And thro' nine channels disembogues his waves
        Here stood her chariot here if Heav'n were kind
                        High on his chariot and with loosen'd reins
                 Twice sev'n the charming daughters of the main
                 Ent'ring with cheerful shouts the wat'ry reign
                        The cheerful blaze or lie along the
ground
                        With cheerful words allay'd the common
grief
    Restore their strength with meat and cheer their souls with wine
                     Ilioneus was her chief Alethes old
  Struck with unusual fright the Trojan chief
Thus while he dealt it round the pious chief
                 Three hundred circuits more then shall be seen
                        Long cited by the people of the sky
        And sov'reign laws impose and cities build
           The people Romans call the city Rome
                        Of clashing flints their hidden fire
                        Clear from the rocks the vessels
with
     With which he drives the clouds and clears the skies
           The dart aloft and clench the pointed spear!
                     Aeneas climbs the mountain's airy brow
        With which he drives the clouds and clears the skies
```

Figure 116 KWIC Example

10.7 Document-Term Matrix

The following program is part of a larger collection of programs written in Mumps for information storage and retrieval (IS&R). The purpose of these is to identify in a document collection those words or concepts which best characterize the documents for purposes of retrieval. The complete set of programs is available at no charge at:

http://www.cs.uni.edu/~okane/

This particular program reads document text and builds (1) a *document-term* matrix, (2) a *document frequency* vector, and (3) a *dictionary* vector.

A document-term matrix is a matrix where each row is a document and the columns are words or terms that appear in one or more documents. The value of a cell in the matrix is, initially, the number of times a word appears in a document. Figure 117 gives an example.

	W1	W2	W3	W4	W5	W6	W7	W8
Doc1	3	4	0	0	1	7	0	0
Doc2	0	2	4	6	0	1	2	2
Doc3	0	0	0	1	1	8	1	5

Figure 117 Doc-Term Matrix (Image)

Where W1, W2, W2 ... represent the words and Doc1, Doc2 Doc3, ... represent the document identifications. In a typical collection of documents to be indexed, the number of documents may range into the millions and the vocabulary into the tens of thousands.

An important goal of an IS&R system is to identify and retain those words that are likely to be important indexing terms and discard those that are unimportant. Obviously, words such as *and, for, to, are, have, ...* convey little meaning. Further, some terms that might appear to be important may actually not be in a specific collection. For example, the word *computer* would likely be an important term in a collection of medical articles where the term is seldom used and unimportant in a collection of articles about computers where it would likely appear in every article.

The goal of the software is to identify the optimal indexing vocabulary and to index the documents to these terms.

In practice, most documents contain very few of the total possible words. Thus, as shown in Figure 117, many cells have zeros. In one real world example where the number of documents was about 300,000 and the vocabulary was about 60,000 words, most articles had about ten to twenty words after processing. Thus, one each row, nearly all the cells had zeros.

The document-term matrix is ideal for Mumps because (1) Mumps has string indices and (2) the cells with zeros simply don't exist. That is, if a document does not have a particular word, the cell represented by the document number and the word does not exist. Nothing is stored there.

The program in Figure 117 reads documents and builds document vectors (^*doc*). It also builds a document frequency vector indexed by words where each element contains the number of documents in which the word appears (^*df*). It also builds a dictionary vector, likewise indexed by words, containing the number of time the word appear in the collection as a whole (^*dict*). These are used by other programs to refine the indexing. See the URL reference above for full details.

Input to the program is by *stdin* and consists of the documents. Each document has been pre-processed and reduced to a single very long line of words all reduced to lower case where all punctuation and special characters have been removed. The first two tokens on the line are (1) the byte offset into the document source file of the original document and, (2) the document number. Document numbers are simple accession counts.

The program in Figure 117 uses two features peculiar to GPL Mumps. The first is the *shell* command which permits a running Mumps program to invoke a system shell and execute a command. The second is the function *$zblanks()* which removes extraneous duplicate blanks from a string. Both of these facilities are available in other implementations although with different names and calling conventions. See your vendor's manual.

Detail of how the program works are given in comments.

```
1    #!/usr/bin/mumps
2    ;
3    ; Delete any prior global array instances
4    ;
5        kill ^df   ; document frequency vector
6        kill ^dict ; dictionary vector
7        kill ^doc  ; document-term matrix
8    ;
9        open 1:"dict.tmp,new" ;* output temp file
10       open 2:"doc.tmp,new"  ;* output temp file
11   ;
12       set f=0 ; flag set to false
13   ;
14   ; repeat block until f is true
15   ;
16       for  do  quit:f
17   ;
18   ; read in a line from stdin.
19   ; if no more lines, set f true and quit
20   ;
21       . use 5 read % if '$test set f=1 quit
22   ;
23   ; Extract words from line delimited by blank and
24   ; place in array w. Quit when empty string returned.
25   ;
26       . for i=1:1 set w(i)=$piece(%," ",i) q:'$len(w(i))
27   ;
28   ; copy docNbr into doc, k is true word count.
29   ; place offset into ^doc(doc)
30   ;
31       . set doc=w(2),k=i-1,^doc(doc)=w(1)
32   ;
33   ; For each word in w(), record in ^doc the doc
34   ; number, the word and the offset from the start
35   ; of the doc j.
36   ; Write to unit 2 the document number & word on one
37   ; line, separated by a blank and, to unit 3.
38   ;
39       . for j=3:1:k do
40       .. set ^doc(doc,w(j),j)=""
41       .. use 2 write doc," ",w(j),!
42       .. use 1 write w(j),!
43   ;
44       use 5
45   ;
46       close 1,2
47   ;
48   ; Execute a shell command. Sort will sort the words in
49   ; dict.tmp alphabetically. Uniq will read the result
50   ; and write to dict.sorted.tmp one line for each
51   ; unique word preceded by the number of times it
52   ; occurred.
53   ;
54       shell sort < dict.tmp | uniq -c > dict.sorted.tmp
55   ;
```

```
56    ; open the file just created for input
57    ;
58        open 1:"dict.sorted.tmp,old"
59        use 1
60    ;
61    ; Read each line from unit 1. Remove extra blanks.
62    ; Place the word count (piece 1) into ^dict indexed
63    ; by  the word (piece 2). This constructs the
64    ; dictionary vector.
65    ;
66        set f=0
67        for  do  quit:f
68        . read a
69        . if '$test set f=1 quit
70        . set a=$zblanks(a)
71        . set ^dict($piece(a," ",2))=$piece(a," ",1)
72
73        use 5
74        close 1
75    ;
76    ; Similar to above. The lines consist of doc number
77    ; and word. The file created will have count,
78    ; doc number and word on each line. The count will
79    ; be the number of times the word appeared in the
80    ; doc.
81    ;
82        shell sort < doc.tmp | uniq -c > doc.sorted.tmp
83    ;
84        open 1:"doc.sorted.tmp,old"
85    ;
86    ; Similar to the above. Read the file just created
87    ; and store in ^doc for each word, the count.
88    ; Piece 1 is the count, piece 2 is the doc number,
89    ; piece 3 is the word.
90    ; create a transpose matrix of the same data (without
91    ; the word position information). This matrix if the
92    ; term-document matrix. Rows are terms and columns
93    ; are documents.
94    ;
95        use 1
96        set f=0
97        for  do  quit:f
98        . read a
99        . if '$test set f=1 quit
100       . set a=$zblanks(a)
101       . set c=$p(a," ",1)
102       . set a2=$piece(a," ",2),a3=$piece(a," ",3)
103       . set ^doc(a2,a3)=c
104       . set ^index(a3,a2)=c
105   ;
106       use 5
107       close 1
108   ;
109       open 1:"df.tmp,new"
110       use 1
111   ;
112   ; For each document, write to a temporary file
113   ; each word.
114   ;
115       set f1=0,d=""
```

```
116     for  do  quit:f1
117     . set d=$order(^doc(d))
118     . if d="" set f1=1 quit
119     . set f2=0,w=""
120     . for  do  quit:f2
121     .. set w=$order(^doc(d,w))
122     .. if w="" set f2=1 quit
123     .. write w,!
124  ;
125     close 1
126  ;
127  ; Sort similar to the above. The output file will be
128  ; lines with a count and a word. The count is will be
129  ; the number of docs the word appeared in.
130  ;
131     shell sort < df.tmp | uniq -c > df.sorted.tmp
132  ;
133     open 1:"df.sorted.tmp,old"
134  ;
135  ; read the file just created and build the doc freq
136  ; vector giving the number of docs each word appears
137  ; in. Piece 2 is the word and piece 1 is the count.
138  ;
139     use 1
140     set f=0
141     for  do  quit:f
142     . read a
143     . if '$test set f=1 quit
144     . set a=$zblanks(a)
145     . set ^df($piece(a," ",2))=+a
146  ;
147     close 1
148     use 5
149  ;
150  ; display the doc-term matrix.
151  ; The modulo operator (#) in the write command
152  ; is used to trigger line feeds after 10 words
153  ; have been written.
154  ;
155     use 5
156  ;
157     set f1=0,d=""
158     for  do  quit:f1
159     . set d=$order(^doc(d))
160     . if d="" set f1=1 quit
161     . write "Doc ",d,!
162     . set i=0,f2=0,w=""
163     . for  do  quit:f2
164     .. set w=$order(^doc(d,w))
165     .. if w="" set f2=1 quit
166     .. write w," (",^doc(d,w),") " set i=i+1 write:i#10=7 !
167     . write !!
168  ;
169     halt
170
     Input looks like:

     123758 108 relative contribution of bile and pancreatic juice
     duodenogastric reflux in gastric ulcer disease and
     cholelithiasis....
```

```
Output (stdout) looks like:

Doc 108
A2 (1) Bile (1) acid (1) activity (1) and (2) bile (1)
cholelithiasis. (1) concentrations, (1) contribution (1) disease
(1) duodenogastric (1) gastric (1) in (1) juice (1) of (1)
pancreatic (1) phospholipase (1) reflux (1) relative (1) ulcer
(1)
```

Figure 118 Document Indexing

11 Error Handling and Messages

Figure 119 gives the error codes from the 1995 standard. Your implementation may or may not use these.

```
M1  Naked indicator undefined
M2  Invalid combination with $fnumber
M3  $RANDOM seed less than 1
M4  No true condition in $SELECT
M5  Line reference less than zero
M6  Undefined local variable
M7  Undefined global variable
M8  Undefined intrinsic special variable
M9  Divide by zero
M10 Invalid pattern match range
M11 No parameters passed
M12 Invalid line reference (negative offset)
M13 Invalid line reference (label not found)
M14 line level not 1
M15 Undefined index variable
M16 Argumented QUIT not allowed
M17 Argumented QUIT required
M18 Fixed length READ not greater than zero
M19 Cannot copy a tree or subtree into itself
M20 Line must have formal parameter list
M21 Algorithm specification invalid
M22 SET or KILL to ^$GLOBAL when data in global
M23 SET or KILL to ^$JOB for non-existent job number
M24 Change to collation algorithm while subscripted local variables
defined
M25 Attempt to modify currently executing routine
M26 Non-existent environment
M28 Mathematical function, parameter out of range
M29 SET or KILL on structured system variable not allowed by
implementation
M30 Reference to global variable with different collating sequence
within a collating algorithm
M31 Controlled mnemonic used for device without a mnemonic space
selected
M32 Controlled mnemonic used in user-defined mnemonic space which has
no associated line
M33 SET or KILL to ^$ROUTINE when routine exists
M35 Device does not support mnemonic space
M36 Incompatible mnemonic spaces
M37 READ from device identified by the empty string
M38 Invalid structured system variable subscript
M39 Invalid $NAME argument
M40 Call-by-reference in JOB actual
M41 Invalid LOCK argument within a TRANSACTION
M42 Invalid QUIT within a TRANSACTION
M43 Invalid range ($X, $Y)
M44 Invalid command outside of a TRANSACTION
M45 Invalid GOTO reference
M47 Invalid attribute value
M49 Invalid attempt to set focus
M50 Attempt to reference a non M-Term window in an OPEN command
M57 More than one defining occurrence of label in routine
M58 Too few formal parameters
```

Figure 119 Mumps Standard Error Codes

GPL Mumps was originally implemented before the standard defined error codes. Figure 120 gives the list of GPL Mumps system runtime error messages. When using the interpreter in Linux, the code returned to the invoking shell is zero if execution was without error or one of the following in the event of error.

```
 1  Multiple adjacent operators
 2  Unmatched quotes
 3  Global not found
 4  Missing comma
 5  Argument not permitted
 6  Bad character after post-conditional
 7  Invalid quote
 8  Label not found
 9  Too many/few fcn arguments
10  Invalid number
11  Missing operator
12  Unrecognized operator
13  Command error
14  Argument list
15  Divide by zero
16  Invalid expression
17  Variable not found
18  Invalid reference
19  Logical table space overflow
20  I/O Error
23  Symbol table full
24  Function argument error
25  Global not permitted
26  File error
27  $Order error
29  <break> at line:
30  Function not found
31  Program space exceeded
32  Stack overflow
```

Figure 120 GPL Error Codes

The normal action upon encountering an error is to terminate the running program and print the error message.

Alphabetical Index

ACID...9
Addition...59
And..39, 62
ANSI..13
Arithmetic unary operators...59
Arrays..19
Assignment operator..59
Blanks..29
Blocks..40
Break..65
Call by reference..54
Call-by-value...54
Close..45, 67
CODASYL..9
Collating sequences..26
Command line parameters...51
Commands..31, 65
COmputer-STored Ambulatory Record...12
Concatenation...60
Contains...40
COSTAR...12
Division..59
Do...44, 53, 67, 81
Else...72
Else command...38
Embedded double quote marks...17
Equals..40
Eterans Health Information Systems and Technology Architecture.......................12
Exponentiation..59
Extrinsic functions...56
Extrinsic variables...56
Follows..40
Follows operators...61
For...42, 72, 81
Format codes..36
Global arrays..20
Goto..42, 70, 74
Greater than...60
Greater than...40
GT.M..14
Halt...74
Hang..74
If...75
If command...37
Indirection..51
Indirection operator..62
Input/output..36
Integer division...59
ISO..14
Job..76
JOSS..13
Kill..77
KWIC..113
Less than..60
Less than..40
Line scope...47
Local arrays..20
Lock...77
Logical values...18
Massachusetts General Hospital..9

Medical Subject Headings..105
Merge...78
MeSH..105
MeSH hierarchy..22
MGH...9
Modulo...59
Multiplication..59
Naked global reference..26
Network Model database..9
New...78
New command..19, 33
Not...39, 62
Not contains..40
Not equals..40
Not follows...40
Not greater than...40, 60
Not less than...40, 60
NterSystems Caché..15
Numerics..32
Nvironments..26
Open..45, 47, 80
Operators...35
Or..62
Or..39
Parameter lists..54
Parameters to routines...18
Pattern matching..61
PDP-7..9
Post-conditional...29, 65
Post-conditionals..47
Precedence...30
Quit..44, 81
Quit..42
Read..45, 83
Read command..36
Relational operators..60
Scope of variables...33
Set..85
Set command...35
Stdin...36
Stdout...36
String constants..17
Subroutines..53
Symbol table..32, 55
Tcommit..85
Trestart..86
Trollback..86
Tstart..86
Use..36, 86
Variables..18
VistA...12
Write...45, 87
Write command...37
Xecute..52, 81, 87
'=...60
 subtraction...59
_..60
-...59
!...39, 62
?..61
'...39, 62
'?...61

'[..40
']..40, 61
']]...61
'<...60
'<...40
'=...40
'>...60
'>...40
[...40
]...40
]...61
]]...61
@...52
@...62
*...59
**...59
/...59
\...59
&...62
&)...39
#...59
+...59
<...60
<...40
=...40, 60
>...60
>...40
$ascii...95
$char..95
$data..95
$data()...49
$data()...21
$device..89
$ecode...89
$estack..89
$etrap..89
$extract..95
$extract()..85
$find()..96
$fnumber..96
$get..97
$horolog...89
$io..45
$io..89
$job..89
$justify...97
$key...90
$len..97
$name..97
$next..98
$order..98
$order()...49
$piece..99
$piece()...85
$principal..90
$qlength...100
$qsubscript...100
$query..100
$quit...90
$random...102
$reverse..102
$select..102

$stack..90
$storage...90
$system...90
$test...39, 41, 72, 90
$tlevel..90
$translate...102
$trestart..90
$x..90
$y..91
$z...91

CPSIA information can be obtained
at www.ICGtesting.com
Printed in the USA
FFOW02n1001200717
37990FF

9 781438 243382